GO-5

A Sports Novel

By

Rick Birk

ISBN no. 978-0-9819964-0-0

Library of Congress categories: Sports. Sports fiction.
Sports events. Coaching. Ball games.

This book is easily available at go5books.com

What People Are Saying About GO-5

"If you dream, and for some reason that dream doesn't come true, don't stop dreaming - start a new dream."

- Lavern Luebstorf - Former Head Basketball Coach,
Brookfield East High School - Brookfield, WI

"This book was a great story of life lessons that can be learned by playing collegiate athletics. Birk's insight into the life of the small-college athlete is something that transcends the generations. I saw much of myself and my college teammates in the stories of the Magnificent Seven. Birk takes it one step farther, though, and surrounds this fantastic story full of solid fundamental basketball concepts with a cloak of human vulnerability. I think that this book is not only a great read for the avid basketball fans out there but an educational read for coaches and players. I can't wait to see what Rick Birk comes out with next."

- Brock Veltri - Associate Head Basketball Coach,
Carroll College - Helena, MT

"*GO-5* is a story of lifelong friends, and the value of never forgetting where you are from and what those special friends mean to you. It's proof that Vince Lombardi's familiar saying of "Winning isn't everything, it's the only thing" isn't always necessarily true. Good friends are hard to come by, and those friendships are worth preserving. *GO-5* shows how rewarding those relationships can be."

-United States Sports Academy

"When you're not practicing,
Someone else is.
Someday you'll meet that person
And he'll beat you!"
—Bill Bradley,
Former Senator, New York Knick

Dedication

This book is dedicated to Coach Lavern Luebstorf. He has served as my mentor and inspiration in providing me with the courage to help others through the work for which I have a passion. He encouraged me to walk tall and lead others by example and, above all, to let my heart be the determining factor in life's pursuits.

Acknowledgements/Special Thanks

My gratitude goes out to the following coaches for their contributions and encouragement on this project:

Coach Lavern Luebstorf

Coach Joseph Terrian

Coach Donald Pick

Coach Hugh Blank

Coach Pete Vercouteran

Coach Dwayne Woltzen

Coach Dexter Reisch

Coach Larry Riley

Coach Charles Parsley

Coach Bo Ryan

Coach Glenn Wilkes

Coach Ted Wilson

Coach Mike Novak

Coach Tom Moore

Coach Denny Fox

Coach Mike Cady

Coach Brock Veltri

Coach Barry Hinson

Coach Kevin Morrissey

Coach Todd Fazio

Coach Matt Elliott

Coach Jim Ellison

Coach Mark Stavenger

Artistic Acknowledgements

A special appreciation goes to the following people for their aesthetic contributions:

John Birk

John Born

Brad Cooper (Cooper Design Studios)

Buffalo Hardwood

Dallas Photoworks

Todd DeAmicis

Jay Gibson

Jason Harder

Aaron Hardt

Adam Hardt

Aune Hardt

Nicole Hardt

Joe Panos

Dan Ryan

Duane Stich

A special thanks

A debt of gratitude goes to the Hilton Garden Inn Park Place—Milwaukee for graciously providing the venue for one of the cover photos.

Prologue

In 1985, Rick Riley and his basketball recruiting class formed friendships at Lakefield College which would last far beyond their four-year careers. Guided by Lavern Lubinski, their outstanding coach and mentor, their associations were destined to transcend the hardwood court. Love, respect, dedication, and good, old-fashioned hard work shaped the "Magnificent Seven." They never lost sight of their common goals and their precious relationships which, in both the short and long term, shape us all into who we are, who we become.

ONE

THE ROAD TO SUCCESS
IS ALWAYS
UNDER CONSTRUCTION

November, 1980

The smell of the popcorn still lingers in my mind. The excitement in the small, cracker box gym in Johnson Creek, Wisconsin, was beyond belief. As eighth-graders, we were on the road early in the season in our only night game of the year, against a very formidable opponent. The game seesawed back and forth, the result not determined until the final tick of the game clock. As I advanced the ball up the court on our last possession, I could feel the vibration under my feet as the ball hit the dead spots in the old, wooden floor. I can distinctly remember the look of disbelief on the faces of Tony, Lee, Dave, and the rest of my Cushing School teammates, as we watched our final attempt roll softly off the rim. We had played a fantastic game, but had come up short against a great team. Our hearts were broken. Later when I arrived home, my brother, who had witnessed the game, told me it had been a tough loss, but something our team could build on. Despite the score, he told me that I had played an incredible floor game and at times had resembled the great Bob Cousy—the ultimate compliment. With those words of encouragement, I could now go on. Yes, yes, I could play this game.

APRIL, 2007

It was a glorious morning, the sun shining, birds singing, the temperature up to 60 degrees. A well-deserved springtime had arrived at last in southern Wisconsin after another brutal winter. I seemed to be moving with more hop in my step.

This was truly my time of year. Like most people obsessed by basketball, I had been as excited as ever by the last few weeks of March Madness. The conference tournaments set the stage for Selection Sunday, in which teams are chosen based on their resumes or bodies of work. This eventually leads to the Sweet Sixteen, the Elite Eight, and the Final Four. Its finale, the championship between Florida and Ohio State had once again lived up to everyone's expectations and demonstrated the importance of teamwork. Five players who had succeeded only a year before had kept their vow to come back and repeat. Not coincidentally, this team was built around a core of individuals not unlike Larry Bird, Magic Johnson, Oscar Robertson, Bob Cousy, John Stockton, and Steve Nash—outstanding passers in addition to great talents. My throat seemed to swell with the annual lump brought on by "One shining moment," the yearly tribute to all the tournament participants.

As a basketball coach at Pewaukee High, my own season had ended a month before. We had enjoyed a fine season, making it to the finals of the Wisconsin state sectional and earning a 21-6 record. As a business-education teacher and coach, I was doing what I loved and loved what I was doing. I was married to my college sweetheart Terry and had two wonderful children.

Recently I began receiving some odd messages that caused me to reflect. Three emails, one letter, a voice mail, and even a postcard had shown up in the course of a few days, all compliments of my former teammates from

Lakefield College. In the nearly two decades since, I had been in contact with only a couple of them. So I was curious: Why now? And strangely enough, in the last few weeks I had been thinking of each one of them as well.

Since I was a child, sports had always been a major part of my life. My older brothers were both athletes. Brothers and parents alike attended our games. We were each other's greatest fans. Dad, a devout Packer fan, had relished Green Bay's great success under the legendary Vince Lombardi. We all cherished those years, with the two Super Bowls, the "frozen tundra," icing on the cake.

Of all the sports Dad enjoyed, however, his favorite was basketball. Dr. Naismith's 1891 invention had undergone dramatic changes, but the requirements of teamwork, running, hand-eye coordination, and ball handling still were its mainstay. The team that meant the most to him was the Boston Celtics, a group that up to this point had accumulated sixteen NBA championships and would soon add another. Dad had witnessed the Red Auerbach era that began in 1950. His stories of the Celtics' teamwork, fast-break style, great players, and championships were etched in my mind. The leadership of Bob Cousy, their Hall of Fame point guard acquired by chance—his name was picked out of a hat—proved to be a key in their quest for greatness. My own favorite point guard in my early years was John Stockton. Dad would say that Cousy was to him as Stockton was to me, as Steve Nash now is to my own son Adam. The Celtics swiftly added quality players—Sharman, Russell,

K.C. Jones, Heinsohn, S. Jones, Schayes, Costello, Ramsey, Havlicek, Cowens, Nelson, Chaney, White, Silas, and Westphal. They basically ran the same system and reloaded with talent. Their success? It was simply irrefutable.

Yet, every dynasty, sports included, must come to an end. Boston's did in the late 70s. Nonetheless, with great management in place, they made one of the most dramatic moves in team history by acquiring the rights to an Indiana State player, Larry Bird, who quickly became the center-piece of the revitalized team. Earning Rookie of the Year honors, Bird found himself on the court with the likes of Parrish, McHale, Henderson, Robey, and Carr—a new dynasty in the making. By this time I was in grade school and could see with my own eyes the style Dad had so long loved and cherished.

From the Cousy era until the late 90s all the home action for the Celtics took place at the famous Boston Garden. Its parquet floor, a work of art in itself, symbolized Boston basketball. Every kid wanted the opportunity, someday, to play on that hallowed court. I remember cutting out strips of paper the size of the parquet and positioning them in one corner of my bedroom, my very own "piece of the Garden." It was perfect, since my Cushing Grade School colors were also green and white. This was an omen, I felt. During my career, whenever I had opportunity to play on a parquet floor, I would try extra hard to honor the Celtic tradition. It was during grade school, in my formative years, that I got the "feeling" on game day. Sometimes days before, I would get this exciting sense of anticipation that seemed near-indescribable. I loved it. Later on, on game days in college, I was known to say, "I've got that feeling" when I bumped into teammates on campus.

Basketball stories forever made the rounds in our household. One that Dad often shared took place a few years before I was born. In 1964, the state of Wisconsin had its own real-life version of *Hoosiers*. A coach named John "Weenie" Wilson brought Dodgeville, a small school located in south-central Wisconsin, to the state tournament in Madison, where all schools, regardless of size, met in one division. Dodgeville had been the runner-up in 1963, and through hard work, team play, and outstanding games by their star players Rick Brown and Corky Evans, was able to defeat a much larger school, Milwaukee North, 59-45. The attention the game drew was beyond belief. Today, this accomplishment is no longer possible, as the state's high school sports have been divided into classes based on school populations. Meanwhile, Coach Wilson was inducted into the Wisconsin Basketball Coaches Hall of Fame in 1979.

Like many kids growing up, we had a hoop on our garage and a cement driveway, along with a wooden, fan-shaped backboard—all constructed, paved, and installed by Dad. We played games year-round. Weather was never a factor. We played in the rain, the snow, the blistering heat. Many times we wore gloves. I celebrated my tenth birthday in late March with a basketball party. I shoveled all morning long to insure the game would go on. We always knew where each crack in the driveway was, where its incline started and tapered off, how to maneuver around the large, leafy elm tree that shaded the court, and how to make low arching shots. I even learned to shoot a fade-away to score against my older brother using the corner of the garage as a screen as I fell back into the breezeway entrance. Our court became a place where the neighborhood kids convened. We'd play long into the night with only a small, single bulb above the garage door. A few times friends left car lights on to allow us all better vision. Because of the excitement and noise, neighbors eight blocks away would remark about our games of the night before.

I was very fortunate to have an older brother to learn from. When we would play, he would always assume the role of coach, ref, opposing team, opposing coach, even cheerleaders and announcer, each with a distinctive voice. I still kid him about being a schizophrenic at such an early age. One time we had our neighbor Louie tape and announce one of our games as a college media project from the vantage point of our garage roof. We were addicted to all sports, yes, but basketball was always the most cherished. I remember taking a trip as a grade-schooler with my oldest brother. We drove out to Arizona, across to Florida, then back up to Wisconsin. In Baton Rouge, Louisiana and Lebanon, Indiana I requested a special stop. I had to take a jump shot on the same turf where Pete Maravich and Rick Mount had done the same.

In 1987, I had the chance to experience Indiana basketball. My friend Jim Elliott was from Elkhart, and our Lakefield college team had made an early exit in a district tournament. We arrived early on Friday and learned that the boy's basketball regional would be held in Elkhart, the next town over from Jim's home. We made our way over, only to learn that the game would be held at a junior-high. My first thought was, "Indiana basketball? How can it be held in a junior-high gym?" How wrong I was! For one thing, we couldn't get in: The game had been sold out. Our only option was to wait until the first morning game was over. If a ticket-holder's team lost, he may be inclined to leave and you could claim the ticket. After only one person came out, I sent Jim in. Fifteen minutes later, a game security officer gave me a pass to stand with Jim in standing-room-only. He knew I was from out-of-state and gave me a break. As we made our way to the balcony overlooking the court, I couldn't believe my eyes: The gym sat over 7,000. Fans on each side were decked out in school colors. With four teams present, the stands were brilliantly hued in four distinct sections that made up the entire lower level. I didn't see one person without a school color. The introductions were incredible, and the level of play even more. I came to understand the meaning of Indiana basketball and its importance and tradition in the community. The most incredible feature was that winners met for a second game on the "same day."

I had been raised in Delafield, Wisconsin, a small town in

Waukesha County, about thirty miles west of Milwaukee. At Kettle Moraine High I was a three-sport athlete—football, basketball, and golf. Summers I played American Legion baseball and worked as a mason's tender for a neighbor and fellow-parishioner at our Lutheran church, William Timm. This neighbor was a hard worker and a man of integrity. I was fortunate to learn a new language—the language of masonry. A hammer was a "persuader," cement was "mud," and the tool compartments on the truck were "pigeonholes." I learned to drive stick just by taking the truck on my own. My boss inspired business honesty and dedication and left me with a lifetime of benefits.

Despite my schedule, I still managed to hone my basketball skills each night for over two hours. Each night without fail local athletes would gather at either St. Bruno's Grade School in Dousman or a Catholic monastery on Lake Nashota. The games were exciting, outstanding, and lasted long into the night. Often we had to sneak our way into the monastery through an open window or by jimmying a door. On some occasions we could spy monks peering at us through a window high above the court. We would pause and look up as if it were time to receive their blessing. Then on the game would go, players no longer burdened with the guilt of illegal entry. To this day I believe that the priests were giving us signs that all was okay.

In high school we had some solid teams, but we never made it further than the final game of the sectional—the same as my present team this past season. With our outstanding point guard, Tim Hemming, we had a high-powered offense that averaged 84 points per game, which allowed me to average 27 points per game as the team's leading scorer.

This drew the attention of Coach Lavern Lubinski at Lakefield College, a Division II school near Kenosha, Wisconsin. Coach Lubinski's program had a solid reputation as a class act. One major consideration in my favor: He viewed players with multi-sport backgrounds as a plus. He felt that a variety of fundamentals and the will to win together had vital crossover effects. Although none of Coach Lubinski's players had ever gone on to the NBA, many had played professionally overseas.

Everyone who plays college hoops hopes he or she has an outside chance of making it to the big leagues. Couldn't each be an overlooked gift or a "diamond in the rough"? I was no different. I had no offers from Division I schools and was thankful that someone saw something in me. Without reservation I took the scholarship. By joining his program, I felt, I would somehow reach my destiny. Little did I know how much this relationship would serve as the turning point of my life.

Since my first class of the day was a prep, I decided to pull off the road at a favorite spot, a bluff overlooking the bold, blue expanse of Lake Nagawicka. Thoughts of my former teammates and coaches had been on my mind all day. I found myself reflecting on their recent messages, on the path I had chosen, on where I was, and why.

TWO

IT'S NOT ABOUT ME—
IT'S ABOUT US

September, 1985

Seated on the shores of Lake Michigan just twenty-five miles south of Milwaukee, Lakefield College was a beautiful setting—one ideal for me, as I always had an affinity for the water. The aesthetics were such that each location on campus had an exceptional view of the lake. The Lakefield Lancers enjoyed exceptional facilities, to include a spacious football stadium and basketball field-house that sat 5,700.

As I look back on my college days, what sticks in my mind is what my teammates and I endured during those years that planted the seeds that have blossomed today. We share so many memories, both good and bad. I will be forever bonded to this group, this team, this segment of time and place. So much of what I am today is a product of these moments, moments so precious and important at the time and yet which now, today, seem dim memories. Our class, the freshman class of 1985, was a collection of high-school athletes from successful programs, each player having statistics that would rival those of any national Division II school. Four of our players had been All-State. As a group, we averaged 21 points and 9 rebounds per game. This *would* be a group who would reach the nationals and bring home to Lakefield the coveted national Division II championship.

I, Rick Riley, 6'3," had been recruited to play 2-man, or shooting guard. I was fortunate to captain the team my junior and senior years. It was in January of my freshman year that I received the nickname "Coach," a nickname I scarcely knew how to interpret at the time.

Joe Sorelli, 6'7," was to play 4-man or power forward. He was from Greendale and of full Italian decent. His parents owned an Italian restaurant "Peppies" which he told me meant "Little Joe." Based on the name, he said that it would be his destiny to inherit the restaurant. He was right: Today he owns and runs Peppies. Having seen the Tom Cruise flick over three dozen times and due to his impressions of Raymond Babbit, Joe had received the nickname "Rainman."

Jim Freemont, 6'5," would be a 3-man or small forward. He came from Kenosha. Additionally, he would be our school's top golfer, which earned him the nickname "Trevino." Co-captain with me our senior year, Jim had the most potential of the group. Currently he works as a bartender.

Dave Cassell, 5'8," was recruited to be the 1-man or point guard. From Dodgeville, he had won a state championship his junior year. To this day, he is probably the funniest person I have ever met. Truly, he missed his calling: He should have been a comedian. To his friends, he is simply known as the "Midget", a name he acquired in his youth as the star player in his Midget League. Dave is now a pharmaceutical salesman.

Mike Andrews, 6'3," was a combo 2- and 3-man. Our only out-of-state recruit, from Naperville, Illinois, Mike was extremely good-looking and popular with the ladies, who dubbed him "Romeo." Currently a news anchor in Dubuque,

Iowa, he has hopes of making it in New York. With Mike, ego has always been an issue.

Rex Conrad, 6'8" and 250 pounds, was recruited as a 5-man or center. From Whitefish Bay, on Milwaukee's east side, he always had a weight dilemma, which persists even today. Nicknamed "King," he works as a controller—and has a large refrigerator in his office.

Last but not least was Craig Sommers, 6'6," who with his chiseled body and stoic demeanor was recruited as a 4-man or power forward. Originally from Madison, he transferred to Lakefield from Madison Tech where he had been a Junior-College All-American his freshman year. Craig did not join us until our sophomore season, which brought our class total to seven. For his strange antics and occasional references to death, he was nicknamed "The Mortician." Strange as it sounds, he currently works as a funeral director.

These were my class, my group. How the name "The Magnificent Seven" started I don't recall, but we quickly bonded as a group, with great chemistry and cohesiveness. Jealousy was by and large absent. We truly looked out for one another.

Coach Lubinski and his assistant, Coach Blank, would serve as our mentors during our time at Lakefield. The relationship a player has with his coaches is extremely important. It determines both his fate and his outlook. We were very fortunate that our coaches readily shared with us their high levels of expertise. One usually copies from his mentors what he feels are traits that lead to success. I was no exception.

Coach Lubinski himself was 6'3" and in top physical shape for a man 58 years young. His hair was graying. He always wore glasses, except when vigorously demonstrating drills at practice. He had played college basketball and, even at his size, had been his school's all-time leading rebounder. In addition to coaching, he taught two courses for the math department. His office near the gym held a huge picture of his long-time idol John Wayne. Coach was highly respected by players, the school, and his peers.

Coach Blank, in his thirties, had played college football as a defensive back. He had a raspy voice, dark complexion, and muscular frame. He was working on his master's degree in physical education and employed in the school recreation center. He, too, was respected. But as an assistant coach he did not carry the authority of "Luby", even though he tried to enforce his power at times. We constantly kidded him, which didn't aid his image. But because he understood us and knew all the jesting was in fun, he was able to become a valuable conduit between Luby and the team. It was a perfect situation.

When our rookie class convened in the fall of 1985, Coach Lubinski told us we would be going on a journey of both mind and body. As I look back, I initially thought the journey would end with graduation. I was wrong. It would continue for a lifetime and be dramatically enhanced by our increased knowledge base, associations and work ethic.

An athletic scholarship has several rewards. We could sign up for classes before the student body without waiting in any lines. We got the classes we wanted every semester. Book availability was never a problem. I always felt somewhat embarrassed about that, especially when I heard other students' horror stories. As a result, I took my classes seriously. I wanted very much to be the exemplary student-athlete, so there could be no argument.

The first day for every college student is exciting and stressful. In my case, even though I had walked to each of my classrooms the day before, I hadn't planned on the student traffic. I was late for two classes. For the second class, I had a legitimate excuse. As I was crossing the main drag, I found myself beside a blind woman with a cane. She seemed very frustrated. I asked her if I could help. I escorted her to the next building on campus and dropped her off at her class. Then quickly I ran to my geography class, to find the main door already shut. I tentatively opened the door, and peered into the large, completely filled lecture hall, absolutely silent. I ducked in, and edged up the stairs to find a seat.

"Halt—right there!"

I paused, and peered back.

"What is your name and why are you late?"

"I'm Rick Riley, and I just helped a blind woman get across the street to her class."

Immediately the class erupted in laughter.

Professor Smith shook his head. "Next time you're late,

the door will be locked!"

Such, I thought, must have been the rationale behind the old saying, "No good deed goes unpunished"?

Through the rest of my years at Lakefield, I never saw that blind woman again.

In late September I met Jim Freemont at an open-gym session where all the potential basketball players would convene three times per week. When Jim told me he liked to play golf, I mentioned that I played in high school. We made plans to play eighteen holes together. Overhearing our plans, Joe (Rainman), a real conniver, thought that a bet was in order. One thing led to another. I found myself entered into my first taste of "strip golf." For every hole played, the loser would have to discard a piece of clothing. We agreed to meet on the first tee with ten articles of clothing. By the time we reached the green on the back nine, the loser would be the one standing nude. After all, late afternoons in the fall were very slow at our local course. We would not be noticed.

Came the beautiful autumn afternoon, in the mid-70s. By the time I teed off on the 14th hole, I was minus my socks, shoes, two wristbands, a hat, my shirt, my pants, and my confidence. Jim had lost only his shirt and hat. I bent over, clad only in my briefs, to ready my ball, and heard a voice.

"Hold it!"

It was the golf marshal, a smirking elderly gentleman who had arrived in a cart.

"Fellas? Clean it up—now!"

We apologized. I dressed. As he was leaving, he threw back, "Jim—how many under are you?"

Had I known Jim's reputation (as a freshman, he would become our school's top golfer), I would have reconsidered. It didn't take long for the story to travel through the dorms. It was quite tough to live down. I guess now you can understand how Jim got the nickname "Trevino."

We were fortunate to have access to the lake. Many homecoming functions were held on the beach, as were rituals such as bonfires, picnics, barbeques, and student competitions sponsored by the school's recreation department. It was a great way to bond with students of different interests. And there were always brave souls brazen enough to test the temperature of Lake Michigan. I had no interest in that.

Looking back, I remember my classrooms, the dorm, the library, and, of course, the all-important gymnasium. However, one of the most important places on any campus is the student union. Ours was no exception. Here students would congregate between classes and discuss anything from the latest sitcom to Plutonian philosophy. Our union was arranged with an expansive sunken pit full of booths and tables surrounded by a railing and more tables around the upper level. Many areas were unofficially designated as sections for sororities and fraternities. Most students sat in the same areas each day.

We were no exception. We had our own large table where some two dozen people would meet each school day. Jokes and crazy times were commonplace. I learned to play Sheepshead and poker very quickly. My "Go Fish" background seemed inadequate. One could easily feel the pulse of the campus in the union. On the bottom floor of the union was a recreation area. Here we could bowl, play pool, or eat at the campus grill. Moonlight bowling was always popular. The upper floor held a ballroom for dances and more formal activities. Often we danced to local bands well into the night.

New students who took over the reins of receptionist at the main desk or information area would became susceptible to the jests of the student body. On numerous occasions, he or she could be heard paging "Horace Apple" or "Willie Maykit. Come to the front desk!"—accompanied by bursts of student laughter. One poor girl must have paged "Ben Dover" six times before she realized her faux pas and burst out laughing herself.

One afternoon in the fall of 1985 Romeo, the King, and I were at our table when an announcement came over the PA: Everyone was to vacate the union immediately. The next thing we knew, campus police were everywhere. Someone had called in a bomb scare. Romeo and I were a few of the last people to scurry out. As we slipped through the door held open by the officer, Romeo blurted, "Oh my gosh!? Forgot something! Got to go back!" Somehow he talked his way back in, and surfaced seconds later with his latest *Sports Illustrated* (swimsuit edition)—the sole purpose of his return. He displayed the magazine to the crowd and received a hearty round of applause. The police just shook their heads. Luckily, the scare was just a hoax.

Trevino was one of the fortunate ones to have a car on campus. He drove a green '78 Chevy. However, it was well known on campus that he had some driving problems. He told me that once, in high school, the police stopped him for inattentive driving. An officer approached the car, saying, "Young man—don't you know enough to use two hands?"

Jim looked at the cop, over at his girlfriend Joan, back to the cop. "Then how am I going drive the car?" he said.

That remark earned him a ticket.

After practice one day we decided to drive over to Muggs, our local hamburger joint, for a burger. Jim said this was his day to set a personal record. I remember clinging to the car door handle as we whisked through town in an attempt to run thirty-one stop signs in a row. Jim said a rolling stop counted and was careful in his effort to eclipse his own personal record of twenty-three. I was glad we had not eaten earlier. At the restaurant I scoured the menu for an antacid.

The next day at practice, Trevino chose number 31 as his practice jersey and complained that our highest number was 55. We laughed. From now on, we told him, you'll get the number zero.

Since business and economics always interested me, I was excited to take Econ 101. The class was held in a hall with a capacity of some two hundred. On our first day, after a brief mention of supply and demand, Professor Torrian took pause. He announced that tomorrow he would show us a foolproof method to become a millionaire. We would *not* want to miss this class.

I was pumped. I couldn't wait for class the next day. When I arrived, I was amazed. The hall was packed, standing room only, with many students I did not recognize from the day before. The professor lifted his hands for silence. The crowd grew quiet. As he began to speak, he unveiled a large graph with "IBM" written across its top. The vertical left side depicted the price of the stock. The horizontal bottom marked a time continuum. He took up a marker, peered into the audience.

"Ladies and Gentlemen, if you really want to become a millionaire? Then BUY LOW and SELL HIGH."

With that, he drew a line following the general angle of the stock moving through time to its much higher price.

"Folks—*that's* how you earn a million."

The crowd looked around, broke into murmurs. *Had* we all been so gullible to think there was an easy way to become wealthy?

It didn't take long for the room to thin out.

One of the most remarkable events happened in one of our huge sociology lectures. Midget and I were sitting in the hall's upper middle section, near the aisle. The professor, Dorothy Wiencek, had warned the student just in front of me to pay attention and leave the girl next to him alone. Yet the student seemed preoccupied. He seemed to pay little attention to her words. With five minutes left in class, the professor summoned the student to the front.

He stood up whoozily, bumping into a jug of wine poised at his feet. As he negotiated his way down, a trail of red wine followed him, step for step. The crowd burst into hysterics. At once he turned, peered back and noticed the trail. Quickly he took a place close before the professor's podium, positioning himself between her and the aisle in an effort to hide the evidence. He apologized profusely and promised to be more attentive.

Luckily, the bell sounded. Everyone stood up and exited in a shuffle that disguised his crime, which was never discovered by the usually astute Professor Wiencek.

THREE

YOU WILL MAKE MISTAKES—
DON'T REPEAT THEM

Each fall the team meet in the gym three times a week for stretching and then a three to four mile run, followed by some pickup games. At Coach's discretion, this protocol was run by our seniors. As freshmen, we quickly learned to be leery of the seniors, especially when Coach was not present. As part of our traditional welcome, we were taken on runs through water, mud, pastures, and over rocks. But on some days, when they felt tired or sympathetic, they would run us through the woods near the campus where, once out of sight, we could walk much of the way. Once, a dummy hanging from a tree with a "Rookie" sign across its chest waited for us. Our Rainman thought it was cool and gave the dummy a high five. We quickly came to realize that this was the seniors' way of bonding with the newcomers.

My freshman year I was very homesick. I thought once practice started I would be all right. However, this was not the case. The third week of practice I couldn't take it any longer. I caught a ride home with a truck driver from Consolidated Freightways, who dropped me off a half a mile from my house.

Come suppertime, my folks were quite surprised to find me home. My older brother had moved out of state. I really missed him and the times we had together. For the first time in my life I had missed a practice, and I started feeling very guilty. My parents consoled me, helping me realize that things were different now, that change was imminent. The next morning Dad drove me back to school.

The first thing I did was to go and see Coach. He listened to my lame excuse, then said, "Practice is at 3:00. Be on time. Oh, and Rick—that'll be fifty down and backs.

I said, "Yes, sir."

After practice that day, I remember wobbling my way back to the locker room. By this time my teammates had already showered and gone to dinner. I noticed a scarf and a tassel hat hanging from the hooks in my locker. A note was attached: "Stay warm," in what I believe was Coach's wife Shirley's handwriting.

At eighteen I was immature, but at this moment I bonded with Coach. I felt that he knew what I was going through. I was now 100% dedicated to his program—hook, line and sinker. I would do anything to help him and our program succeed.

As the days went by, it became apparent that Coach always knew everything we were doing on campus. It was the strangest thing: How could he possibly be in two places at once? We were convinced that there must be hidden cameras on campus.

One such incident occurred in late 1985. The last day of school before Christmas break, I was hanging out in the Union with Romeo. We were bored. He got an idea. With a little coaxing, he convinced me to join him in standing by the main union door and greeting every girl who came through with "Merry Christmas!" and a kiss. The idea was that we would each take every other girl, no matter who she was. We would keep score until we each had 100 chances.

For the next forty-five minutes I tried to be as appealing as possible. I ended up 98 for 100, and Romeo 94 for 100. One of his victims happened to be Professor Wiencek—and he succeeded! Turned down only twice, I had apparently been indoctrinated into Mike's world and had beaten the best. For years after, I kidded him about that statistic. If I could have had that percentage from the line, I would have traded it. That afternoon at practice, Coach divided the team in two for an inter-squad scrimmage. When he called our names, he referred to Mike as "Smoochy" and me as "Hot Lips." That's all he ever said, but it was enough to embarrass us both: Somehow he knew.

Each semester our dorm had some crazy, wacky competitions. My floor decided to enter a contest to cram the most people in a Volkswagen and drive it the required distance. We had one person steering, another on the gas, one on the brake, another with his head sticking out of the sunroof barking directions to the three who had no view. With a total of fourteen students, we drove the bug the required block and won. Some complained because we gave full body credit to the Midget, one of our participants.

Most nights after practice, the team would walk the four blocks from the gym to the school cafeteria, where we would eat as a group. This was the highlight of the day. The manager, a lover of sports, made sure the kitchen stayed open late enough to accommodate us. It was an all-you-can-eat deal. We would eat, talk, eat, talk, eat, talk, and laugh for hours.

One night my brother John was visiting me at school. We had just filled our plates and assumed seats at our normal spots. All at once we sat dumbstruck. A girl came strolling by on her way to the kitchen. She was absolutely beautiful, extremely shapely—to be very blunt, very well endowed.

We decided that on her return trip past we would get to know her. As she strode by with her refill of Coke, we stood and gave her a vigorous round of applause. She paused graciously, laughed, and joined our group. She was very poised. To be honest, some of the guys had not figured she'd be so articulate. She was Barb Davis, from Racine, a double major—history and Russian. In high school, she told us, she had been a foreign exchange student and visited Turkey. Upon her return to the States, some officials thought her group had contracted a communicable disease and quarantined them in New York City for five weeks. On a bet with fellow students, she sneaked out and applied for a job as a Playboy Bunny. With a fake ID, she was hired and worked part-time for a month. She said the experience was unforgettable. As she recounted, she had the captivated attention of our whole group. Right then and there we coined her "the Bunny"—a nickname she liked.

I dated the Bunny a few times as a freshman. No matter where we went, there came the double-takes—definitely not due to my good looks. One weekend the Bunny came home with me and some of my other friends to meet my parents and share pizzas. My parents had planned to go out with another couple for the night. For some reason it took Dad some two hours to leave the house after being introduced to Barb. Mom was upset. Barb had that effect—especially on males.

As a freshman, when you hear of opportunities from your coach, you weigh them seriously. Coach Luby was always looking for such prospects for his players. After practice one day he contacted Romeo and me with an offer—a campus modeling job. We would report to the head of the Art Department— Mr. Henry Febrantz—the next day at 1 p.m. We would model for an hour and receive $15 each. Coach added that the class would be sketching human models.

We arrived at 1 p.m. sharp. We quickly noticed that the class was made up of coeds and the star of the Art Department, Professor Febrantz' protégé, Sam Evans. As class started, the professor told the class to take out sketch pads and chalk. He turned to Romeo and me in front of the class.

"Okay, fellows—you may disrobe."

"Excuse me?" I managed.

"You knew this was nude modeling, didn't you?"

I turned to Romeo. Already he had his shirt unbuttoned and was breaking into a strutting striptease. I humbly joined in, but only down to my underwear. When Romeo was down to the gold jock strap he had donned for the occasion, Professor Febrantz said that we could now pose.

Romeo assumed the posture of a statue of Adonis. My

own contribution consisted of both my hands covering my package. It was the longest class I ever had—at Lakefield or anywhere else.

That night we had a home game. Entering the locker room for the usual pre-game talk, Coach showed an odd look. He surveyed me, then Romeo.

"How did the art gig go, fellows?"

I started to chuckle. Suddenly I heard Romeo—"Coach, this is what they got."

He stood up and unveiled two sketches from art class lying against the chalkboard. The room broke into laughter, but within a minute Coach had us refocused on the task at hand.

Many coaches have a variety of stories to motivate players. Al Maguire, former coach at Marquette, related one of the best at a banquet: "One time I was in a restaurant having dinner. Because I loved seafood, I decided to order lobster. When the waiter brought my dinner, I noticed that one of the claws was missing. I asked him what the deal was. He told me that this sometimes happens—when the lobsters are still alive they fight in the tank. I told the waiter to take my lobster back and bring me a *winner*."

Coach Luby, too, had such a gift. One of his methods during the season was to display a new axiom daily on the board in the team room. The first I saw was:

**THE ROAD TO SUCCESS IS ALWAYS
UNDER CONSTRUCTION.**

The seniors had told us to expect this every day. Coach

was unique. His dry humor wasn't always understood. He especially relished "Ponderings by George Carlin," which he worked into his messages. As each new axiom would appear, we would seek its deeper meaning.

To bring more levity to the locker room, our class decided to develop a rating system. We split the sayings into four categories—*M* for motivational, *O* for just plain odd, *T* for making us think, *H* for humorous. We rated each on a 1-5 scale: 1 for low quality, 5 for high. Because the letters spelled *MOTH*, we called the process Mothballs. A great, funny saying was an H-5 and a sub par, odd one was an O-1.

For the last practice before Christmas our freshman year, the day's saying was:

CHRISTMAS IS WEIRD. WHAT OTHER
TIME OF YEAR DO YOU SIT IN FRONT
OF A DEAD TREE AND EAT FRUIT
AND CANDY OUT OF YOUR SOCKS?!

It earned a score of H-4. When we came in from practice, hanging from our lockers were socks draped in our team colors and full of candy and fruit. Each proclaimed, "Ho Ho Ho!" We knew, again, it was the work of Shirley.

In early January of 1986 we met to prepare for our game against St. Andrews. The saying for the day?

THE DIFFERENCE BETWEEN ORDINARY
AND EXTRAORDINARY
IS JUST THAT *LITTLE EXTRA*.

Coach seemed in a superbly upbeat mood. Previously

he had listed on the board all the special plays we would use in conjunction with our motion offense—Go 5, In, Counter, Invert, Spud, and Henway—and now he appeared in his favorite blue suit and gold tie, matching our school colors. After we took our seats for our pre-game talk, he scanned the room as if to make sure each of us was present. I had heard from older teammates that Coach would sometimes act unusual to calm the team down in tough situations. With rugged St. Andrews, I thought something odd might be in store. I was not disappointed. At the end of his speech, he slowly resurveyed the room. He focused his sights on the Midget.

"Dave, do you feel comfortable running all these plays? Do you know your responsibilities on each one?"

The Midget looked up at the board. "Coach, I can run them all with no problem. But I've never seen that one. What's a 'Henway'?"

Coach looked at Dave. "About two pounds," he replied.

The room burst into laughter. The Midget had just had his initiation. Would I be next?

We felt loose, played great, and went on to win, 79-68.

Late my first year, I was a bit upset to receive the nickname "Coach." Did the guys think I was too pushy? Too brown-nose? As time went by, though, I felt that I had built trust, and saw the name as a great compliment to my character and knowledge of the game. Having that nickname made me strive for perfection, to do all I could for our team's success.

Collectively, our rookie group did not get a great deal of playing time. We understood that we were in the business to win games against stronger, more experienced opposition. The Midget had talent, but in playing taller opponents became quite foul-prone. One night he exited a game after having played three minutes and committing three fouls. In disgust he took his seat at the end of the bench and slipped into his warm-ups. Within two minutes, Timmy Wiencek, our starting point guard (the sociology professor's son), committed his forth and fifth fouls, and Luby quickly re-summoned Dave. Dave dashed to the scorer's table, was buzzed in, and ran out onto the floor. Everyone, including the refs, failed to notice he was still in his warm-ups. Dave was in a stalwart defensive stance, pressing full court, when a whistle blew. Sheepishly he shed his warm-ups, and walked them to the bench for disposal, to applause from the crowd.

"I was cold," he managed.

Even Coach got a chuckle out of that one.

In a nutshell, our first season was an exciting one. We were senior-laden, but incurred several major injuries. After we started out 15-6, two of our players went down, so I was able to start eight games and Trevino six. Each of us made giant strides in our ability and effectiveness. The team struggled to a respectable 19-10. It was a learning experience for all, the primary benefits being the level of play and length of the season. As Al McGuire put it, "The best thing about freshmen is that they become sophomores." That is true: With age *does* come experience. Next season was something we all looked forward to.

Coach seemed to intuitively know my inner struggle. I loved basketball but had no idea what I was going to do with my life. What would I major in? Where would I work? I enjoyed my business and economics courses thoroughly but could not picture myself wearing a suit and tie and working 8-5 each day.

Coach always encouraged his players to move toward whatever each had a passion for, really loved. Life is too long to be unhappy, he would say. One day he took me aside and told me of a new major the school would offer. Under the direction of the business and education departments, it would be a specialty program called "business education." This, he was sure, would fit me like a glove. I would be on the cutting edge of a new enterprise of which I already had a solid knowledge. I could help young people. He even mentioned the possibility of my coaching.

That conversation, one sunny afternoon in the fall of 1986, changed my life and is the basis for what I am today.

FOUR

A GOAL IS A DREAM
WITH
A DEADLINE

October of my sophomore year brought another life changing event. Rex and I were playing cards in the Union. Two new girls came in to sit at a nearby table. We went over and asked if they would care to join us in a hand of poker. They agreed, and we introduced ourselves to Terry Bishop and Jean Frost.

We decided to wager. Confident they didn't understand the rules, we felt safe. The losers would have to clean the others' rooms. It didn't take us long to win. I set a time for Terry, and Rex did the same with Jean. The next night, right on time, Terry knocked on my door. "Cleaning crew!" she announced. She worked hard. In no time my room was spotless.

More importantly, it was the start of a lifetime of love.

Terry was a freshman nursing major. She was a knock-out and a high-school valedictorian. It was always Terry's goal to graduate from Lakefield in three years. My teammates thought I was the luckiest guy alive and referred to Terry as "Fox." After a few weeks, we went to her home in Kenosha. Both her parents were one hundred percent Polish and extremely Catholic. The large family of eleven children were very hardworking and middle-class. I was in awe of her mother—such a genuinely spiritual person. I knew that the acorn does not fall too far from the tree and I hoped that would be the case. It was. Today Terry works as a neonatal nurse, spends her life helping others, and absolutely loves her job.

Rex, too, was always thinking of others. Sometimes, however, it seemed to spill out onto the basketball court, as he received some flack for not using his size and strength to take advantage of opponents. Coach wanted to improve everyone's leadership skills and often called our group "The King and His Court" in an effort to spur Rex to take charge. Coach did what he could to build confidence in the King, but, as he would say, you can only *lead* a horse to water.

Yes, we all had our strong points, our specialties, our weaknesses. Rex's? Rex's was food. He *loved* food. Often we tried to calculate how much money the cafeteria was losing because of him. On road trips Coach would usually turn to the King to choose the appropriate dining spot. This led to many jokes, for the King would usually pick a restaurant with an all-you-can-eat menu and plenty of ribs, steak, and shrimp.

Dating was not one of Rex's strong points. He was always a bit shy. I remember the struggle it was just to get him to meet girls—like the day we played poker in the Union. When he did go out, the date would usually be the first and last. The guys would ride him amusedly with comments like, "Who's queen for the day?" This scarcely helped his confidence. He would laugh along, yes, but I knew he was frustrated. As often as I could, I would set him up to double with Terry and me.

By the time our second year came around, we felt we had a solid handle on the program. Everyone had made great strides from the year before. We were a relatively young team—two seniors and two juniors. At the start of the season Coach reminded us tradition does not graduate. Because of our strong beliefs and habits, we would remain successful. Trevino, Rex and I started and had good years. However, we were on average nineteen-year-olds playing twenty-one-year-old opponents, a discrepancy that makes a considerable difference. Also, we had an extremely tough schedule. As a result, we struggled to a record of 14-14. Our inconsistent play was a huge factor. We dazzled with some great halves, played mediocre other halves. Quickly we found that at this level such was not enough.

In January, 1988, I heard on the radio that my boyhood idol, "Pistol" Pete Maravich, had passed away. So often I and countless others had tried to copy and emulate his style on the court. Many thought he was a showboat, too fancy at times, but he had a confidence and flare that set him apart. He imprinted his own style, but it was not without resistance—including that of some of his coaches. He played at Louisiana State University for his father Press at a time when freshman were not eligible for varsity. Remarkably, he averaged 44.2 points per game for three seasons. Drafted by the Atlanta Hawks in 1970 as the number-3 pick and receiving a bonanza of money, he was traded to New Orleans four years later. In all, he played a decade, his last year (1980) with Larry Bird. In one game he scored 68 points against the Knicks and was a five-time All-Star. In 1996 he was named to the NBA'S 50th Anniversary All-Time team. After that, he walked away, having never won a championship. He died doing what he loved—playing a pick-up game at age forty.

Another sport that I enjoyed was ping-pong. In February of my junior year I entered our all-school tournament. The first two years I hadn't gotten up enough courage to enter, but Rex and Romeo were entering and insisted I do the same. Since my experience included fifteen years in our garage back home and family tournaments, I felt I couldn't embarrass myself too much. I knew I could beat both the King and Romeo and was the best ping-pong player on the team.

As the tournament proceeded, I seemed to get better with each match. I made it to the semis, where I would be matched with the King. The other semi-final to be played right next to us at the same time was between Masahisa Amano, a foreign exchange student from Japan, and Sam Evans, the Art Department protégé and apple of Professor Febrantz's eye. The whole art class, including Professor Febrantz, was there to cheer on Sam. These were the same people that had seen me in my underwear only a few years earlier. I wondered if they would envision me the same way?

Both matches started at the same time and drew good crowds. At one point, just after one of our points had ended, a ball came bouncing over from the other match. Rex walked over to retrieve it for Masahisa. The King's foot got stuck in the carpet. He lunged. Amid a large crunching sound on the tile, the ball vanished from sight under one of Rex's size fourteens. The crowd broke into hysterics and cheered for a full minute.

The 250-pound Rex was speechless. He reached down, picked up the eggshell remnants of the ball and handed them over to Masahisa. "Sorry," he said. Again the crowd broke into laughter.

Masahisa ended up beating Sam 21-9 and 21-14. As for Rex, who was not the same after the incident, I was able to defeat him 21-14 and 21-12. In the final match, Masahisa prevailed 21-14, 19-21, and 21-16. I didn't feel bad. I played the best I ever had. Masahisa was a heck of a player.

We entered our junior years with great optimism. With eight out of our top ten players returning, we were ready to take control. We were a deeply experienced team, a factor to be dealt with. Already we had played six games in the summer during a week-long trip to Ontario. We seven went along with two seniors, Ed Wackendorf and Matt Nelson. We went 6-0, along the way defeating a fine all-star team from several universities in the last game. The country was beautiful and we enjoyed the fishing and swimming. Rex, who hooked a 36" musky the last day, was by far our best angler. After we had secured the fish in the boat, he told us how vicious muskies can be and of stories of muskies attacking humans. We asked him: Why had he waited till the last day to tell us—after we all had been swimming only a few hours before?

Our junior season opened with us clicking on all cylinders. We won our first six games and ended with a 23-7 record. Our last contest was a late-March, 83-81 overtime loss to Milligan to decide who would represent the Midwest region at the national tournament. That left only one year for the Magnificent Seven to fulfill the dream. The years were going by too fast.

The next summer I worked again for my neighbor and did not miss one day of basketball training. I was determined to fulfill my dream of a championship. The Lakers had defeated the Pistons 4-3 in a very exciting series. We all felt that, despite the loss, Detroit would be a force to reckon with next year with their bad-boy style. Rumors were flying throughout the sports world about potential blockbuster trades. In August came the news: "The Great One," Wayne Gretsky, would be going from the Edmonton Oilers to the L.A. Kings. This was one of the major trades of all time, involving perhaps the best player to ever put on hockey gear.

When school started in the fall, it seemed as though the song "I Heard It Through the Grapevine," earlier popularized by Marvin Gay in the 60s, was resurfacing to honor these rumors. The TV version had anthropomorphized raisins dancing to the notes. It was hard to believe that this would be my last fall at Lakefield. I wondered what would be next for me. Had Lakefield been the right choice? *Would* the grass have been greener at another school? I was finishing up a quality education. I had a great coach, friends, and teammates. But we hadn't yet reached the nationals—the measuring stick of success.

Our senior-year squad consisted of the Magnificent Seven—Joe, Jim, Rex, Mike, Craig, Dave and me. We also had two freshmen guards, the Weber twins, Andy and Chris, from Brookfield. Tom Kastenholtz was a freshman guard from Milwaukee Messmer. Ben Rennicke was a freshman forward from Grafton and the younger brother of Midge Rennicke, our head cheerleader. David Kenney, a junior center, was from Fox Point. Tommy Engle and Charlie Sileno were two sophomore forwards that had played together at Homestead High School in Mequon. Ludwig Bub, an exchange student from Milan, Italy, was a junior point guard.

It wouldn't be fair to fail to mention our team trainer and our manager/statistician. Trainer "Big Mike" Barnes had contracted with the University to be available for all practices and home games. Mike was quite the character. About 6'2" and weighing 275 lbs., in his early forties, he had played a year of football at Lakefield and admired Coach Luby. Our manager/stat man, Everett Schellneffer, had been with the team all four of my years. We were lucky to have him. Due to his efforts, all was ready on time— water, uniforms, practice gear, equipment and supplies. More importantly, Everett was a math/computer genius and thereby a perfect fit for Coach. Ev had taken the job mainly because he had been designing a sports-computer program for basketball since his freshman year and wished to gain better insight into the game. Very industrious, he tutored some of the guys on trips.

By the second semester of our junior year, Ev's program had been refined to a product better than anything on the market. Its results were available almost before the team retired at half-time to the locker room. Claiming it to be far better than anything he had ever seen, assuring that it made a night-and-day difference, Coach urged Ev to push his idea. Right after graduation in May, Ev flew to Everett, Washington, to receive an official offer from Microsoft— and has been a mainstay of that company ever since. I guess you could say he truly found his 'window' of opportunity.

My own degree in business education required that I practice-teach a semester. I chose Kenosha Tremper High School, near the Lakefield campus, the first semester, so that it would fit in more smoothly with our season. The time and effort was rewarding. I quickly gained appreciation for the teaching profession and how to keep a large group not only under control but motivated. You never know how you will teach until that room door closes for the first time and leaves you in charge. Young people need a consistent set of rules to adhere to, and each teacher must decide which is more important—to be liked by the students or to provide those often unpopular rules that provide students the chance to gain the most in knowledge and character. Having been under Coach's wing for three years, I naturally chose the latter. Coach was a master teacher in his own right. When I was given the tasks of teaching and coaching later in life, I felt a huge responsibility to give my students and players *correct* information. I had to know and understand whatever

I was talking about. Fortunately, I had received solid fundamentals to help me in this process.

To say the least, Craig the Undertaker differed from most of us. He would burn incense in his locker that was covered with pictures of dark silhouettes. We kidded him about having a doll he could stick pins in. He lockered next to Joe, who for the most part, always seemed to have nagging injuries. Joe's ointments and Craig's incense created some strange smells. A bit of a loner from a broken family, the Undertaker loved to work out. The strongest player on our team, he could easily have done a Soloflex commercial. He also seemed more serious than the rest of us and spent much time reading on road trips. I probably got to know him the least of anyone, but I knew he respected me. Several times over the years he had my back.

Each year after the team had been pared down to size, we would get our uniforms. Dave forever had a problem. Ev would hand the jerseys out and tell us each to pick a pair of shorts from a pile he left on the training table. During this particular year, Dave had been last to the locker room, having come from a late class. There was only one pair of shorts left.

We had already gathered in the gym for a team picture when he emerged from the locker room holding his waist and very upset. "This *isn't* going to work," he said.

Mike was arranging everyone for the team picture. "What's the problem, Cassell?" he asked.

Dave glared over. "These would be too big even for

you!"

With that, the Midget released the shorts, which promptly tumbled to the floor and left Dave standing with just his jock on. We virtually fell on the floor laughing.

"Yeah—and we can't even put him in the back for the picture!" Joe quipped.

In November, 1988, George Bush the Elder was elected President of the United States, defeating Michael Dukakis, Governor of Massachusetts. Bush was replacing an incumbent, Ronald Reagan. Who could ever have guessed that his son George would someday serve our country in the same capacity? Two songs—"Simply Irresistible" by Robert Palmer and "Get Out of My Dreams and Into my Car" by Billy Ocean—were high on the charts. With Romeo providing the locker room music, we heard them constantly, and would all sing along.

FIVE

PROPER TRAINING OF AN ATHLETE IS A FINE HABIT TO ESTABLISH FOR LIFE

Coach Lubinski was one of the most highly organized people I have ever met. Besides his witty sayings, he provided us with daily handout "hints" about basketball. Well thought-out, these tips would aid any player's mental preparation. Because they were so logical, players bought into his philosophy swiftly. (I have appended some of these hints in the index section of this book).

Coach's practices were methodical, mapped out to the minute. I can't recall one that did not contain several fundamentals and explanations of their importance. When a player finally understands the justification for organization—its streamline of efficiency and tangible results—he tends to not only accept the routine by the numbers but to embrace it as part of himself.

No one ever wanted to receive a call from Coach. Because he was so organized, it would be something completely out of the ordinary. We were young, and always feared: Wouldn't it have to be bad news? To complicate this was the fact that you could hardly hear Coach on the phone, he spoke so quietly. As a result, we named him "The Soft Talker." When he did call, it was embarrassing to have to constantly repeat, "What did you say" or "What was that, Coach?" After a time, we would just agree with his mumbled words and hazard the most logical guess. We always wondered: Had we let him down in some way? I sure wish there had been email back then!!

At the start of each season, Coach would assemble the

team to present his self-actualization/leadership speech. We referred to it as "Luby's Hierarchy of Needs." Its graphic version was usually placed on the board in the locker room, just below the daily saying. It consisted of a large pyramid partitioned into five horizontal levels. Alongside each level was the calculated number of victories to be achieved by fulfilling the needs of that level. At the base were the most fundamental needs. On the way up the needs became more sophisticated. Level one: With our talent this year, just by showing up and playing a little man and zone and running our motion offense we could earn 9-10 victories. Level Two: This included a strict defensive philosophy involving pressure on the ball, on the line—up the line help defense, proper block-outs, furiously rebounding, chasing every loose ball. We could expect to win 13-15 ball games. Level Three: We would have our offense down to a science. A combination of our patented motion offense and twenty-five specials would allow us to solve any defense we faced. Also, we must be always willing to share the basketball, stay open-minded, and read what the defense would give us. This would yield us 18-20 victories. Level Four: Earmarked by attitude which would create cohesiveness, this demanded that each of us give of himself for his teammates at all cost, along with an undaunted positive attitude, proper communication, and a game face despite any circumstance. This would bring us 23-25 victories. Level Five: This top or apex level revolved around intangibles. Coach would have to do a great job of coaching and keep us both confident and hungry. The home crowd must be involved. No player would be afraid to look at himself in the mirror to bring out his best. We would all manifest our belief in our system and take responsibility for our actions. We would play for the name on the front of our jerseys and not the number on the back. Lastly, a bit of luck wouldn't hurt. Executing all these actions would guarantee a 28-plus-wins season. The sky would be the limit.

We would have this speech each year just prior to taking the floor for practice about a week before our first game. That practice was always incredibly spirited and intense.

Freshmen and newcomers to our program were expected to pass an exam at the start of each season. Coach felt that a player should always have a good understanding of basic basketball information, to include court, backboard, rim and ball dimensions, basic rules (periods and timeouts), even the teams in our conference. The veterans always tried to overemphasize the test's difficulty, equating it to an SAT, as a way to indoctrinate the young players.

We were always expected to give the same effort at the defensive as well as the offensive end of the court. If we did not, we would hear about it pronto. When we thought of defense, said Coach, we should think of blue-collar workers and should each pack a hard hat. He didn't want any "Matador defense" allowing our men to blow by us without moving our feet as if we were saying "Olé." Ultimately, we were protecting the "Castle" (the basket), and "our defense must surround it as if we were a moat." To fortify this, we worked daily on our techniques such as slides, run and catch, tracing the ball, help and recover, and boxing out from all areas of the court. This constant pressure would cause our opponent to falter or miscue into making errors or getting happy feet (traveling).

Taking a charge is not popular with players, but each week we practiced the techniques and positions which would help us perfect this skill. A proper stance was the key to staying in front and with your man. We employed a defensive strategy called the "Baseline Dive." Initially we would force the ball out of the middle of the court and toward the sideline. There we would overplay our opponent and invite him to go baseline, to trap and harass him with our shifting help defense. We would initially show them the baseline and then take it away. The idea was to keep the ball from being moved side to side, which would deny our opponent improved offensive opportunities. Coach never wanted us to leave our feet when defending a jump-shooter. He wanted us to have our hands up—straight up—challenging the shot. "You can't leave your feet—they're attached," he would say. "So don't leave the floor, either."

There are always times in a game when momentum is key and a defensive stop is crucial. Whenever we heard Coach yell "Lancer, Lancer, Lancer!," we needed to step up our defense and, no matter how tired we were, dig down deep and assert ourselves to the max.

Of Coach's many unique traits, one was his vocabulary. I will never forget his use of the phrase "the particular situation" when referring to a point in time during a game or in our lives. He *coined* the phrase. In describing and naming plays, he would do so in an effort to make it easy to remember and at once describe the action to a tee. Many times he would employ math equations or terminology. The crossing motion of players was X, the flip-flopping of our big and small players INVERT. He would call a lob over the top for our 5-man KAREEM. A back-door alley oop dunk for our smallest player the Midget was SPUD. He would produce equations—e.g., attitude + talent = efficiency. Often he would refer to the toughness of Hondo, or, as he would say, John Wayne. He also loved acronyms. One day he wrote BEEF on the board. Rex was getting noticeably excited, until Coach explained that this had nothing to do with food but was the formula for a great shot in basketball: balance (solid stance squared up to the basket), eyes (eyes on the rim), elbow (keep elbow straight), and follow through (finishing your shot).

Each year a night or two before our first game, to jumpstart our season, we would hold our annual pizza party. We would congregate at Luby's house, a short block from campus. Shirley always made sure that everyone had enough food and drink. For the party of twenty there were always at least a dozen pizzas of all types, and plenty of soda. Joe felt that, if it was Italian food, you couldn't go wrong. Shirley would always serve a huge chocolate cake for desert with, of course, ice cream. As soon as everyone had his fill, Coach would give a short talk—not about the season, but about everyone just having a good time. However, he would say it was his duty to acquaint us with what he thought was the greatest movie ever—*Hoosiers*. Then he would promptly show it. We would all enjoy the film, but Coach couldn't help but break in at times to point out fundamentals and philosophy similar to those of today and our current team.

Coach would always say, too, that basketball was a game of disguise. Sound, proper fundamentals can overcome size discrepancies. Smartness can often overcome athleticism. Block-outs, changes of pace and direction, ball fakes, one-on-one moves—these give a player enough confidence to take on a more seasoned opponent. He would point out that great shooting nights could mask a team's other major deficiencies in defense, turnovers, or rebounding. Luby would say, "Hey, I disguise myself as a basketball coach. I'm just a math teacher who happens to be in a gym." He also felt that no job was beneath him. With assistant coaches and managers available, he would sweep our floor each night and help prepare our practices with water and equipment. Players, coaches, managers—all were equal in his eyes.

Coach's IQ and propensity for math related to his helping us understand the importance of angles in basketball. Where our big men posted up, where our wings made entry passes, the screens we set for teammates—these were all facilitated by employing proper angles in relationship to the basket and specific spots on the floor. Luby wanted our wings to be extended at the foul line, our big men to post above the block. The strategy was to move the ball side to side in the offense to create these angles and catch an unsuspecting defender on the wrong side, which would give one of us a clean shot.

We should understand all elements of the game and positions on the court. In this way we would know first hand, for example, the problems involved in posting up or delivering a proper entry pass and appreciate what a teammate was going through. Too, some of our big people had nice outside shots and many of our smaller players good post-up moves. One technique Coach used was to position our big people on the wings and our guards on the blocks. This was one example of what he called INVERT (reciprocal in math). This set usually succeeded, as our opponent had rarely planned for it or had their players ready to defend each area of the court. Yet, I'm quite sure that in four years we never called an Invert when Midget was on the wing!

Once Coach entered the locker room for the pre-game talk, music stopped. All the chat fell away, and we would take our seats immediately. It was our responsibility to have read the daily saying. All the players had the utmost respect for Coach. We valued his ideas, values, even wishes—all necessary ingredients of an organization's cooperation and success. We never feared Coach. Fear is imposed on a person; respect is earned. Coach would visit the locker room before us and outline his game plan on the board. This outline would comprise the basis for his talk.

At the start of each year, Luby would have us memorize a series of events that would occur on a standard trip up and down the court—"The sequence." He might test us on this, he warned, and anything less than 100% would require extra running. But in all my years, he never ever tested anyone.

Prior to our Marian game, early in the season, Coach came into the locker room and spied "The Undertaker" with a paper sign taped to his forehead reading "Test Me." Coach glanced around for an explanation. Finding none, he looked back at Craig. "Test Me?" he asked.

As if on cue, Craig stood up and yelled out: "Sir, the order for the day is defensive stance, ball pressure, help defense, on the line—up the line, arm in passing lane, contest shot, secure rebound, make outlet pass, fill the lanes appropriately, keep good spacing, set solid screens, secure great scoring opportunity, 3, 4 & 5 crash the boards, sprint back on defense with head turned and back in defensive stance."

With that, he sat back down, seriously, and unpeeled the sign from his forehead. The whole room fell into hysterics. Coach, too, showed a grin. "Craig, I applaud your effort, but you were starting tonight anyway," he managed. "And by the way—it's 'successful outlet pass.'"

One of the things I learned from Coach was the importance of saying thank you to your teammate for a pass that led to an assist and a chance to score. When time permitted, we would point to the teammate in appreciation. "Sharing is caring," he put it. When Coach gave a compliment on a successful shot, he always mentioned the passer. If he thought you were hogging the ball, he'd say, "How many teammates have pointed at you lately?" This made for a team atmosphere: *Everyone* wanted a compliment from Coach. He was quite clever about this.

One night we were playing Beloit and the Midget made probably the best no-look pass I have ever seen on a 4-on-1 fast break. Happening right at the end of the half, the pass resulted in an alley-oop dunk for Craig and a ten-point lead. All four of us stopped like we were frozen in time. Collectively, we pointed at the Midget. It was an awesome sight.

Coach Luby seemingly had an answer for anything. If a game turned really intense or momentum swung in our opponent's favor, he would call a timeout and set up "Pressure Release." Because the opponent was hyper and excited by his success, he would tend to overplay on defense in an effort to take charge and thus would become suscep-tible to a counter-play. We would run a backdoor cut off our motion offense for a lay up or an alley-oop lob for a dunk off a weak-side back screen (Spud or Go Blast). To disguise our strategy, we would run this play from our regular motion set. Timing, patience, execution—and, most importantly, a slight sense of arrogance in the foe made this work.

Possession of the ball was always a huge factor in suc-cess— enough to be a fundamental by itself. You can't score without it; the "other guys" can't score if you have it, Coach would say. So get possession, keep it, pass it, possess it with all your might. How your team handles the ball tells if you are a high-class team. A team in possession of the basketball and understanding what to do with it is in no danger.

SIX

FAILING TO PLAN
JUST MIGHT MEAN
YOU ARE PLANNING
TO FAIL

Each practice, after our stretches, we'd move to ball-handling. We'd slap the ball, move it in circles, do figure-eights around our legs, waists, necks. We would do the same on the dribble, adding stretch dribbles, suspending the ball, and ending with a spider drill. Then we'd do cones set up at designated spots on the floor. One after another, we would approach the cones and plant our outside foot and push off and step in the opposite direction with our other foot. This would aid our ability to change direction. Next, with a basketball, we'd make the same moves—a crossover dribble, behind the back, through the legs, finally the spin move. It awed us to see our gradual improvement. Even our big people—Rex, Mike, Craig, Ben, David—gained so much confidence through these drills, confidence which, Coach assured us, would allow each of us to develop unique moves to break down an opponent and gain separation. These moves would set the stage for each of us to own a buffet of shots and opportunities. Coach wanted us to work on all moves, yes, but each of us should try to master two or three that could, as he put it, "break anyone's ankles." My own favorite became the stutter—inside-out crossover that lets me, even to this day, free myself on virtually any occasion.

The next phase was a shooting drill. Coach suggested that we view the front of the rim for consistency. The drill lasted five minutes: one minute and fifteen seconds from each of four spots—the two elbows and the two baselines, fifteen feet from the basket. We had two lines—shooting and passing. Once a player took his shot, he would retrieve the ball, pass it to the passing line, and take his place in that line. The drill required three balls. After the minute and fifteen seconds had elapsed, Coach would yell "Next Spot." We would all rush there. The idea was to be able to ready oneself to catch and shoot as swiftly as possible. That this required a solid pass became very obvious. As we made shots, we would yell out our total. Our record, my junior year, was 133.

Coach knew first hand what hurt a team wasn't the physical mistakes but the *mental* ones. He never grew upset if anyone missed a shot. He knew well that any player would try his hardest to score. It was part of our DNA. What *could* be corrected was the shot chosen. Any mental mistake in practice drew a player a "bonus". Coach would point out the error and you would be on your way—down the court and back at full speed.

Once, in the heat of competition, Joe traveled on a routine fast break. He didn't come to a two-foot jump stop and, as result, dragged his pivot foot. Joe set the ball on the floor, ran to the baseline, and sprinted two bonuses. We all watched in wonder. As Joe returned, Coach replied, "Joe, we only require one bonus."

Joe looked at Coach. "Coach–one for each foot," he said.

We chuckled. That's the kind of dedication our team had, starting with Coach Luby. Episodes like this brought levity to our practices and added to our cohesiveness. We learned that one sign of a solid player was the ability to "play through" adversities like travels or air balls. Mental toughness was the key.

We also learned quickly who was in charge. Envisioning only a top-notch program, Coach required that we be under control at all times. More generally, our ability to manage on-court pressures would help us prosper and grow. No cursing was permitted. I never heard Coach swear. If a player did cuss, the whole team was put on the line and had to run. The strategy was that the other players would be upset with the offender and that the pressure would quickly shape him up. It worked. I remember a practice when two players cursed. Not only did we all have to run, but the next day Coach showed up with an appropriate handout list of terms to use if frustrated. These included darn, oh fudge, nuts, shucks, gee whiz, gosh, gosh darn, jeepers, jeepers creepers, oh boy, golly, golly gee, rats, sun of a gun, shoot, holy cow, crumb and fuddy duddy. We all got a kick out of his list, and it had its desired impact. Several of the guys even used some of the terms, which amused us all.

Most importantly, this control element must carry over to the games, especially in reacting to the referees. Those in stripes we treated with utmost respect, no matter what the circumstance. In my four years, Coach never earned a technical foul. He would remind us: When the ref handed us the ball to inbound or shoot a free throw, we must say thank you. If the ball ended up on the other end of the court, nearly always one of our players retrieved it. Officiating can vary game to game, and we learned to adjust to the refs' lead and to accept their decisions without protest. Coach explained that, in the long run, this behavior would work to our benefit. Often it did. We had far fewer issues in this regard than most teams. Respecting teammates was a major key to our program. Complimenting them became second nature. During games, not just the five playing but *everyone* was in the huddles. Even when our bottom five were on the floor, everyone was involved and cheering for each other. It was all about respect.

Coach believed that, without a doubt, the most underrated fundamental in the game was the ability to pass the basketball. This he must have told us hundreds of times. Basketball was a game to be played without ego. The open man would get the ball. We worked on our passing drills daily—hook passes, bounce, chest, wrap around, lobs, and skips were all part of our routine. Coach stated, "Show me an unselfish team and I'll show you a team with far more options and weapons." A passing team was a happy team. Passing should be done with *quality*, not as a last resort when a player's personal agenda was on hold. This game is a team game. Sharing is truly caring.

Coach's announcement "Everyone on the baseline!" meant that practice was nearly over. After the sprints, he would survey us and announce that he needed two free throws, a rainbow three, and two dunks with attitude. "Who are my participants?" he would ask.

We would confer and send our best shooter to the line. Similarly, whoever had been hot that day was designated to shoot the three. The Undertaker was always assigned to take care of one dunk; it was up in the air for the second. Since the penalty for missing an attempt was a team bonus, concentration was all-important. Last, each player would shoot a free throw; we'd all run if we did not make the required 13 of 15 shots. Again, this was a team-building time, and practices usually ended on a high note.

You need a plan to finish tight games. Instead of going into a freeze, a stall, or a four-corner offense that could prematurely halt his team's aggressiveness and maybe cause it to play not to lose instead of to win, Coach employed another strategy. He ran our usual offense somewhat tightly, emphasizing getting either a lay-up or an uncontested fifteen-foot shot. This would require that players set absolutely perfect screens for teammates, come to meet the ball when receiving a pass, and keep the correct spacing at all times. This strategy, called "Melt," he had learned from a Coach Fox in Alaska. We melted the clock, but kept ourselves open for chances to score. This way we play to win instead of not to lose—a huge difference. To see such control at the end of games almost always result in success was a real confidence-builder. Screening itself was an important fundamental. Coach always referred to the great Indiana teams coached by Bobby Knight as instances of how to set screens. When such a player set a pick, he would jump-stop and at the last moment would lean and step in the direction of the defender attempting to stay with his man. Many times a ref might view this as a moving pick, but the way such teams subtly pushed the envelope was an art in itself.

Our bread and butter was our motion offense and ability to pass and move the ball. Coach's philosophy worked to prevent empty possessions. We didn't want to turn the ball over and always worked to get open shots. Free throws and second-chance points were an additional payoff. Our motion offense had a few rules regarding whom to pick or where to cut. Once we understood these rules and our basic system of operation, our team spacing improved and our shot opportunities grew rapidly.

However, a four-and-a-half month season brings occasions when the foe seems to have all the answers and overplays your patterned cuts. As back-up, teams have special sets and plays unfamiliar to opponents. After all, didn't Coach tell us that basketball was a game of disguise? The idea was to get the foe to react in an unaccustomed manner and make a poor decision that would give us opportunity. Our fast break included several options. One option moved the ball quickly down the court without the ball touching the floor. Coach called this "Red." We players dubbed it "Jiffy Lube." We had at least twenty special-set, half-court plays a season. Some were made for specific players, some for a two or three-point shot, all with an eye to the shot or game clock. But of all these special plays, "Go-5" was Coach's favorite. We ran it when we had a desperate need to score. It would involve a back pick and a double screen that could give us either a lay-up or an uncontested jumper from the free-throw area. We would practice it at least three times per week.

Our senior campaign started very positively. We won our first four games (although three were at home). Coach tried several lineups and finally settled on Dave, me, Jim, Craig, and Rex at positions one through five respectively. We felt that we now had not only the athletes but the experience to meet our team goals of a trip to the nationals and a national championship. Of our twenty-eight games, sixteen would be at home, a big plus.

We were also fortunate to draw huge crowds. Over three thousand students living on campus helped our cause, but we also had a secret weapon or an ace in the hole—the "South 40." This was a group of the most boisterous, obnoxious students on campus. They actually held tryouts. In the group were more than a few football players, and all were led by infamous Doug "Koo Koo" Keller, an all-conference linebacker who some thought had been administered one too many hits on the gridiron.

The group occupied the seats right behind our opponent's offensive basket. They would shout, tip beach balls to each other, hold up signs, display pictures of girls in bikinis, scream and yell in unison or individually, make barking noises—anything to distract our foe's concentration. On one occasion, as the other team was being introduced, the South 40 all held up newspapers as if they weren't interested. As if these antics weren't enough, the group was allowed to trade seats at halftime and seated themselves on the opposite side of the court under our opponent's basket for the second half as well.

Teams who were otherwise great often folded at the free-throw line when harassed by this group. If by chance a player missed his first attempt, it took real guts and concentration to convert the second. For all they did, the South 40 should have received our yearly "Sixth Man" award.

Every year our team participated in at least one charitable activity. This year we worked at a local homeless shelter to help provide Thanksgiving for over a hundred people. We practiced from 6:30 a.m. until 8 a.m. and then rode out to the shelter and stayed until 2 p.m. It was an eye-opening, worthwhile experience. Everyone appreciated our help. Coach let us leave at 2 p.m. for our own families' dinners as well. It was a win-win situation for all. During each season, Coach had a friendly wager with our women's basketball coach. Very simply, the two would compare team cumulative grade-point averages at the end of the semester. A trophy would sit in either his office or the office of the women's coach. During my tenure we were about fifty-fifty. This competition made for some humorous times and friendly barbs between our two teams, but, most importantly, sent us a useful message about the significance of study.

Romeo always had a way with women. On trips, Joe would always say that we had to keep him on a very short leash. He loved to meet opposing cheerleaders. Often we would find him deep in conversations with them as if he had known them for years, as if they were long-lost friends. It didn't take a brain surgeon to figure out why he got such huge rounds of applause when introduced on the road.

The closest I ever saw Luby come to getting a technical was in our sixth game, against LaCrosse. It was a tough game that went back and forth. The lead must have changed at least two dozen times. It was tied, 72-72, with twenty-two seconds left, when the ball went out of bounds. The refs didn't know whose ball it was and huddled together to confer. Because we had no timeouts left, Coach shouted, "S-O-B!" to our team on the floor. The refs turned to Luby in disbelief: Was he describing *them*?

Coach smiled. "'S-O-B': SIDE OUT OF BOUNDS," he explained, our choice of formation to inbound the ball. The refs laughed, and somehow awarded our team the ball. We in-bounded and ran "Melt." Craig hit a jump hook with two seconds left to steal the victory.

With another road trip on the horizon and the semester quickly coming to a close, I was feeling lonely and missed my family. However, I realized that in just a few weeks the holiday season would be here. Coincidentally, I got a good-luck call from my mother just before a road trip. She sounded sad. Roy Orbison had died, she told me. Music pioneer and icon Roy Kelton Orbison's work had long been a part of our culture and family. I remember hearing "Only the Lonely" and "Oh, Pretty Woman" so often at home with my family. I still enjoy his music today. My own kids were weaned on his songs on my cassettes.

When Coach gave a compliment, he meant it. Earlier he had been at a basketball clinic held by Bo Ryan, head coach at the University of Wisconsin—Platteville, a Division III School. Coach reported that he had never been so impressed and predicted a stellar career for Ryan. As of the 2007 sea-son, Coach Ryan had amassed over 500 career wins. He left Platteville after fifteen seasons, spent two at Wisconsin-Milwaukee, and then moved to Wisconsin-Madison in the Big Ten. To date, he has won four D-III national titles, was four times Division III Coach of the Year and Big Ten Coach of the Year in 2002 and 2003. An author of several books and instructional videos, he intro-duced his patented "Swing" offense as a sterling example of passing and screening. During my years at Lakefield, we did not face Platteville, but as a coach myself I have utilized his offense several times. It stressed passing, screening, teamwork, and making the opponent work during every pos-session, allowing less athletic teams to compete at a higher level. Coach's prediction about Ryan's impact on basketball was accurate.

Every year we played our neighbor to the north, Campbell College, and this year it would be on their turf. It was only a twenty-minute ride, so we piled into two vans to save money. This was usually a grudge match that gave them a chance to duel a D-II opponent. We had won every year, but the games had been feisty and competitive. This one was no exception. The saying for the day was:

**ATTITUDE AND MISTAKES WILL
DEFENSE YOUR TEAM MORE
THAN ANY OPPONENT.**

As we loosened up, we were hitting an incredible percentage. Everyone was absolutely on fire. As warming up can sometimes breed overconfidence, I was hoping our shooting proficiency would carry over into the game.

As visitors, we were introduced first. Then, as we departed the floor, the lights went out. A spotlight fell on their players. As their names were sounded, the crowd went crazy. The lights flicked back on, only to reveal that their fans had hurled dozens of eggs in our direction. Eggs were everywhere, even dripping from the high ceiling. The refs had to delay the game twenty minutes to clean up. After the game began, the eggs high on the ceiling continued to drip, causing more delays. The announcer warned the fans. The Campbell coach implored the fans. What a few had thought was humorous had now become dangerous. Despite the eggs, we remained focused and hit our first five shots. At the end of the half, Rex even attempted a three-pointer for the first time. He had no green light to do so, and claimed he did not know where he was on the floor when he let the shot go. His ball banked off the backboard and went in, prompting a loud cheer from the team and our crowd.

On our way to the locker room for the half, Rex high–fived the Campbell mascot in front of virtually everyone. Coach quickly pulled him aside: He might have thought it was funny, but it was a slap in the face of our opponent. It could have serious ramifications in the second half.

While we hit 62% in the half, Coach was upset. "Great shooting, guys, but if we weren't shooting so well we'd most likely be down," he put it. He mentioned that Rex would now receive the trophy at the year-end team banquet for the highest three-point percentage for the season, because he is *not* going to take another for Lakefield again. That comment drew smirks from several players, but not from Rex.

Sure enough, our eighteen-point lead quickly dissipated. We let them back into the game. For us the basket seemed to have a lid on it. Conversely, they had renewed confidence. We had to pick up in a hurry because they had nothing to lose by playing their big brother down the road. Jim just missed a fifteen-footer in regulation, which would have won the game. Then the Midget hoisted a half-court shot, with no time left, to take us to a second overtime.

The game ended on a play I will never forget. We were down by one point with 2.7 seconds left and had to take the ball the length of the court. Trevino had fouled out, so I would be taking his place as the in-bounder. Rainman and the Midget were to face me and station themselves on the elbows, fifteen feet from me near the other team's basket. At the center of the court would be Romeo. Rex would position himself at the far free throw line, near our own basket.

Coach had taught us that after a made basket we could legally run the baseline and even step back from the out-of-bounds line. Campbell predictably put their tallest player, a 6'8" center, on me to impede my view and success for a long pass. Their other players locked up man to man as well. When the ref handed me the ball, I took a step back to create some space. The only way I could get the ball down court was to throw a hook pass before five seconds elapsed.

I wound up, faked a hook pass. The huge defender bit— and leapt high. On his way back down, I recoiled and now heaved my hook pass. The ball came off my fingertips with much more arch than normal, and I had to be careful to gauge the height of the gym ceiling.

I was shocked to see the ball sail over his outstretched hands, and raced out onto the court to see the result. At the other end, Rex leaped high and came down with the ball securely in his grasp near the free-throw line. He pivoted, released a turnaround jumper which hit the rim and bounced off to the left. Just as he released his shot, however, Romeo streaked past the King, jumped high, stretched out his hand, and tipped the ball onto the backboard and through the basket. This we had accomplished with still two tenths of a second still on the clock. This *had* to be the best play of our college careers.

In the locker room we went bonkers. We asked Rex what he had thought when he missed the shot. He told us the first thing that had come to mind was, "Wherefore art thou, Romeo!"

He had definitely gotten his answer.

We left for the jovial trip back to school. Coach drove the first van with the seniors, Coach Blank the trailing van with Mike, Ev and the others. As we got up to speed on the freeway, a car pulled up to our driver's side. Its interior lights went on. Its windows descended. We all thought it was strange. Then we realized the two girls sitting in the back and front had lifted their sweaters and were flashing us.

"You guys *rock*! We love you! Go, Lancers!"

We tried to stay calm, to no avail.

The worst part was that Coach had viewed the whole thing—just as we had. We were embarrassed for him. The car then slowed, to give our younger teammates behind the same show. Yells and whistles erupted.

Coach was philosophical. "You know, sometimes life throws us curves," he said. "Take a deep breath or two and try to maintain your game faces."

He said this with what seemed to be a slight smirk. We all cracked up. *Had* Coach been young once, too?

It was a night I will never forget.

SEVEN

IF YOU ARE A SUB—
BE THE BEST SUB
POSSIBLE

It takes a special woman to be a coach's wife. To be a great coach, you *need* that special woman. Coach Lavern Lubinski and his wife Shirley were a perfect team. Never in a million years did I ever think I would play for "Lavern and Shirley." Shirley understood the game as well as anyone. She also understood that the best way to play the game was with vigor and class. Her cheering could be heard all through the game. She was a positive role model for us, no matter what the circumstance. She took an interest in every player and all of our our girlfriends. Many times she could be seen sitting with them. They seemed to migrate to her.

Remarkably, Shirley always found time to do special things for the team and still teach second grade (for thirty-four years). She accompanied the team on about three road trips a year. She always had gifts for us—it was like having a second mom. Both home and away, she would sit exactly four (Coach's favorite number) rows behind our bench and urge us on. Shirley and Coach never had children, but they did the next best thing. They were "surrogate parents" for hundreds of students through the years.

About three times each year we would be away from home on a Sunday. If that were the case, Coach would take us to church. It was not required, but most did go. Coach was a practicing Catholic, but he pushed his faith on no one. In fact, he would take us to services of diverse denominations—I remember Lutheran, Presbyterian, Jewish, and Baptist, to name a few—for the experience. The more ideas we encountered, he thought, the more solid a base we would each build for future decisions.

We all enjoyed our roadtrips, especially the King. To this day I believe he has the school record for pounds of chicken eaten during a single team meal. On the way home from North Central College in Illinois, we stopped at Ray Bussler's, a restaurant offering an all-you-can-eat chicken dinner, which Rex chose immediately, as did most of us. I believe the count came to thirty-nine pieces that he devoured in the hour we were there. We exited the place clucking like chickens.

By law, the team bus had to come to a stop at each railroad crossing. Whenever a RR sign appeared in the distance, Rex would yell, "Here comes a Rick Riley stop!" The first three times were funny. After that the routine, unlike Rex's dinners, got old.

One of the great road trips was going up to River Falls for the holiday tournament, usually the weekend before Christmas. In the last three years we won this tournament twice. With students still on campus, we drew decent crowds. When we played a very tall team, Minnesota-Morris, with four people over six-nine, Luby told us, when among the redwoods in the paint, to box them out and lean on them with our butts in an effort to make them reach over us. To offset their size, we had to press most of the game and keep them from slowing the game and setting their offense. Early on they took their time, using their big people as pass receivers. But eventually they ran out of patience. At one point in the first half, they failed five times in a row to get the ball over half-court in time or threw the ball away. We coasted in the semi-final and beat them by a score of 84-71.

In the final, we met Bethel College, a great team who had made it to the nationals the year before and had returned with their nucleus. Very well coached, Bethel was a team similar to ours in size. They started five seniors. Like us, they passed the ball extremely well and didn't settle on questionable shots early in the shot clock. This was a blue ribbon caliber game. Each team brought its best effort. At any point throughout, there was never more than a six-point difference. With twenty-four seconds left, Bethel hit an elbow jumper to tie the score. After a timeout, we ran our two-guard zone offense, gap movement against their two-three zone. Rainman's twelve-foot bank shot from the right wing, with four seconds left, gave us the lead for good, 82- 81.

We scampered into the locker room chanting "Rainman! Rainman!" Joe smiled, hoisted his hands high as if to hush the crowd. With that famous, demented look on his face, he proclaimed, "Joe Sorelli likes swish! Joe Sorelli likes swish! Who's on first?"

At this, we busted up. He was truly our Rainman. We all knew what was slated next—a stop at the famous Westwind, the all-you-can-eat buffet/smorgasbord of prime rib, steak, shrimp, and fish. Rex was in ecstasy. We all gorged ourselves. The Morris team was there as well, which gave us a chance to meet some of their players. It's odd how different guys behave when not dressed in their uniforms.

We left the Westwind both happy and stuffed. On the way out, we passed the board listing the entrees for the evening. The Undertaker took a piece of chalk. With it he drew a careful line through each one. At the bottom he scrawled, "Sorry—temporarily out everything." He signed it "The King." We all rested comfortably during the six-hour ride back to campus, even happier after hearing the news that Trevino, Craig and I had made the all-tournament team.

Our next game, at home on the following Tuesday, was against Augustana College from Illinois. We were fortunate to have the Milwaukee Bucks' dance squad perform at halftime. The score was tied 38-38. We headed for the locker room. Holding his groin, Romeo stopped at the trainer's table at the end of the gym, groaning, "I'll just be a sec. I think I pulled something."

As he lay on the table we all filed past into the locker room. During his "treatment" he had a perfect view of the halftime show. When it ended, he miraculously recuperated, his groin as fine as ever, and he and big Mike rejoined the team. The second half, Romeo did not play much, however. We all knew the lesson he learned and how he regretted such a rash decision. Meanwhile, we won by fifteen.

On his limited budget, Coach Blank did not have a vast wardrobe. On a night prior to one of our games, he had left his brown blazer in the locker room while he watched the women's game. As we readied ourselves for Coach's entry, Rainman picked up the coat and put it on. In a raspy voice he said, in a way only Joe could say," Coach Blank like defense. Who's on first? Yah, Coach Blank wants victory." Though Coach entered to find us all in near-tears and unable to contain ourselves, Joe had finished his routine just in time and had laid the coat back in its place.

The Saturday before Christmas, the Midget and I were invited to a surprise birthday party for Cindy Westbrook, a senior turning twenty-one. Since the invitation included a guest, Dave and I took Terry and Ann. It would be a festive, dressy occasion. Suits and dresses were in order. Dave and I picked up Terry at her dorm, then made our way to Ann's home near campus. As Ann exited, she and Terry were quick to notice that the two were wearing the exact same dress and shoes— an incredible match. Dave and I laughed, but the girls found it all but amusing. We dubbed them the "Double- Mint Twins" all night and mixed their names up several times, on purpose.

When we arrived at the elegant Seven Seas restaurant on the eastern shore of Lake Nagawicka near Delafield, we were taken into a spacious, rustic private room overlooking the lake. We could order anything we wanted off the menu. At night's end a huge cake was wheeled out to the table. We all sang "Happy Birthday." Cindy's dad appeared and handed her a small package. She opened it, discovered a set of keys, and looked oddly to her dad. "Turn around," he said. As she did, the curtains parted. Spotlights beamed down on a spanking new, baby-blue Mustang convertible. She screamed. We, too, were in shock. The Midget leaned to me. "For *my* birthday I got *five bucks*."

It was another night we would not forget. We took the Double-Mint Twins home. I got out of the car to say good-night to Ann. The ladies didn't find the joke funny. I believe neither has forgiven us to this day.

Just before Christmas we traveled down to Chicago to play Melrose College, a small, private college in a tough area of town. This, too, was a night not easy to forget. Of all the rah-rah speeches, signs, and motivational ploys Coach had made through the years, this one would top them all.

Melrose's teams were always talented and extremely athletic. This year they were 15-2 and ranked 4th nationally in Division III. We came into the game with one day's rest, after a victory over Ripon. A big win here would allow us to all go home and enjoy the holidays. With a 14-3 record we were feeling pretty good about ourselves.

The game started very fast, and the action was incredible. Within seconds, they were all over us like cheap suits. Their press was suffocating. We had practiced against it the day before by using seven people on defense. We should have used ten. Within seven minutes, we were down by eighteen. With thirteen minutes left in the twenty-minute half, we were out of timeouts. We had used them in an effort to curtail their momentum.

Coach was beside himself. I don't think any coach, even Luby, could control himself in such a loud, hostile environment. Now I understood the importance of the South 40. I wished they had come along. We managed to be down only by nineteen at the half, on a three-pointer by me and a last-second tip by the King: We had scored the last five points.

Coach led us back into the old, musty locker room. Tension hung. Sweat blotted his shirt under his favorite blue suit and gold tie. He grabbed a ball. "The particular situation is this," he began and elaborated, "We're giving the game to them. I thought we were beyond this! Above all, we must *maintain our poise*. Gentlemen, we need to be the aggressors. When there's a rebound, it's *our*—" he pointed to us—"ball. Loose *ball*? You must go after it like there's no tomorrow!"

He then rolled the ball down the aisle between our two benches. Incredibly, he raced after it. He leapt through the air. For a moment he appeared suspended in air. He landed— on the ball. Securely he grabbed it, rolled it back and forth with a death grip. "This is *my* ball! This is *my* ball!" he screamed.

With that he got up, carefully brushed off his pants, and handed the ball over to the Midget. Without a further word, he turned and left the locker room. We were in shock. Then everyone broke into hysterics.

Coach Blank was left to deal with the situation, but had little success. He was as shocked as we were. None of us heard a word he said. As we took the floor for the warm-up before the second half, we could see the blotches of dust and dirt on Coach's suit. He had done all he could. Now it was our turn.

The second half wasn't any easier, but we were much stronger with the ball and cut our turnovers in half. This gave us more shot opportunities, and we scored more readily. With their full-court style, the pace was staggering. We were exhausted by game's end. While we did draw within striking distance—down by only two points with two and a half minutes to go—we lost, 87-81.

For weeks after, we talked about the game and Luby's halftime antic. Several of us mimicked the leap. What a coach *won't* do to motivate his team? We had a great deal to mull over during our break.

After reporting back on January 2, we had two practices a day for three days and one on the fourth day. Coach had urged us to play during our time off to stay in shape, and we had. On the 6th we left for Northeastern Illinois, a major college and a golden opportunity for us. We got on the team bus and took the two-hour trip to Chicago.

To this point, we had to have been one the most organized teams in the state. Our assistant manager, Ned Stevens, was taking Ev's place, who was not yet back from the holidays. After arriving, we went directly into the locker room to dress. As Ned pulled the uniforms from the bags, we all noticed a terrible stench. The uniforms were stiff. They had been left in the bags under the bus since the night of the Melrose game.

As we slipped into them, pandemonium erupted. They were hard, crusty, smelled like outhouses in hot summer.

The guys were screaming someone had cut off their air supply! Already Northeastern had our names and numbers flashed on their scoreboard. There was no way to change. We decided to take the floor to appease Northeastern. The problem not only made it difficult for us to warm up; the refs ruled the stench "unbearable." They sent us back to change into some practice uniforms Northeastern had kept in storage for several years. We took the floor like refugees. None of our numbers matched those on the scoreboard. Our jersey fronts read "EAGLES" (Northeastern's nickname). All night we would hesitate before passing to a teammate, as the uniforms seemed so out of place. Simply, the "real Eagles" outplayed us. We lost, 89-74, and did not look good. We never did learn who caused the uniform debacle.

As the second semester started, I felt a sense of uncertainty. This would be my last semester at Lakefield. My practice teaching was now behind me. I had no idea where I might end up. However, I was fortunate to go out the way I came in. I had started my first year with Professor Torrian's Introduction to Economics and now I had him for my last economic course, Money and Banking. He was a great teacher; he related well to the students and could point out the ethical ramifications of business and economic activity. January, 1989, also marked the one-year anniversary of the death of Pistol Pete Maravich. I couldn't believe it had already been a year.

On January 20, 1989 George Bush, Senior, took the oath of office, placing his hand on the same Bible used by

George Washington back in 1789.

Whenever I think of January of 1989, I think of *Twins*, starring Arnold Schwartzenegger and Danny DeVito. As a team-building outing, we saw the movie in Kenosha and enjoyed the trials and tribulations of Julius and Vincent. I don't know *how* many times over the next few months I heard the famous line, "I like nuked food." Romeo confessed: One of the female leads, Marney, was *hot*. We all agreed. As we were leaving the theater, Joe took pause for a moment, and then announced: The Undertaker and the Midget should have auditioned!

Each January and early February provides us with a new NFL champion. In 1986 we were invited to a huge Super Bowl party at Midge Rennicke's house in Grafton. Midge, the captain of our cheerleaders, invited the entire team, all the cheerleaders, and their guests. Midge's parents hosted the party and put on an unbelievable spread. As for Midge, she was one smart lady who would graduate and then go on to medical school in Milwaukee. She now works as an obstetrician in the Milwaukee area. Terry and I still hear from her each year. She's married and still lives near her parents in Grafton. As for the game, San Francisco beat Cincinnati by a score of 20-16 in Miami. The great Jerry Rice was named the Most Valuable Player. None of us knew at the time that this would be the last time Bill Walsh would coach in the NFL.

EIGHT

IF YOU THINK ON THE BASKETBALL COURT, IT'S TOO LATE. TO BE EFFECTIVE, YOU MUST REACT

When you think of Wisconsin cold, you think of one thing. When you think of Northern Michigan cold, you think of quite another. In late January, we headed up to Marquette to play Northern Michigan University. The weather was a frigid ten degrees below. I don't ever remember being so cold in my life! While Coach insisted that we all take along the appropriate apparel, I don't think anything would have helped. We could hardly wait to get to the motel, which was more like a lodge. It was rustic, with a wide lobby boasting a huge fireplace in the center. Its most unique feature by far stood in one corner of the lobby—a twelve-and-a-half-foot, thousand-pound grizzly bear.

Its huge claws, open mouth, razor teeth, and authentic appearance left us in awe. Simply, it seemed alive. No matter where we stood, its piercing eyes seemed to take us in. To show he had no fear, one of our sophmores, Chris Weber, jokingly poked several pencils in the animal's rear. The antics got a laugh, but we seniors decided to teach him a lesson. At the pre-game meal, Chris found himself seated next to the Undertaker—a figure a little intimidating to a freshman to begin with. Craig recounted a legend. Indians always buried bears after they had killed them or had found them dead, out of a sense of security and respect. The legend held that an unburied bear's remains would become a constant "call of the wild" to others to come to its aid whenever someone defiled its corpse or place of death. As Craig spoke so intensely, I believed he was relating what he felt was fact. His words were scaring not just the freshmen but *all* of us.

As we left for the game, by coincidence I bumped into Mr. England, the father of my girlfriend back in eighth grade. He had been so supportive of me through the years. He did business here twice a year and was staying at our lodge. "What do you think of the bear?" he asked. "Awesome," I replied. With this, he wished us good luck and bundled up to leave.

The arena was large and only half full. Northern was a quality team and hard to beat at home. I was assigned to guard Max Adams, the nation's eighth-leading scorer. Warming up, we noticed one of their players had "BEAR" as a last name on his warm-up jacket—which made our freshmen a little uncomfortable. As I stared at the jacket, I caught a familiar face in the stands. Mr. England grinned, and gave me a firm thumbs-up.

We played a solid first half. I held Adams to eight points. The game was very up-tempo. Both teams were playing at a high level. At halftime we trailed, 44-40. Despite the zero weather, Northern turned up the heat in the second half, shooting a remarkable 62%. Adams finished the game with thirty-one points, making his last five shots. They coasted to a 91-79 victory. The game took its toll in other ways, too. Rex and Mike sprained their ankles. Jim got a minor hip pointer.

After the game we ate pizza in our motel lobby. The

younger players didn't say much. Afterward we headed to our rooms for a good night's sleep and an early start in the morning. As I passed the bear, I noticed: The pencils were absent.

It was good to get home, where it was thirty degrees warmer. We really needed home cooking, and the thought of our own beds and the South Forty was appealing. Two nights later we would meet notoriously tough Carroll College from Waukesha. The problem was that Mike, Rex and Jim were still unable to play. Coach always seemed to know what to say in tough situations, but this would truly be a test. We were down to twelve players: Two of our starters—and three of our top six—were out.

Coach explained that this was a great chance for us to prove how deep Lakefield was as a team. We can take freshmen and sophomores and put them in our system, as guys like Mike, Jim, Rex, Joe, Dave, Rick, and Craig will give them encouragement, direction, and confidence. They'll be able to step up at any moment and bring their best.

This was great psychology. The younger members felt confident; the older players felt obligated to give them positive feedback. Each group executed just what Coach had hoped they would. We all took the speech to heart and played a terrific game, winning 81-74. Our young people did answer a curtain call. Freshmen and sophomores contributed ten rebounds and four assists and an amazing twenty-six points.

Two days later we were back on the road, this time traveling up to Milwaukee to play the UW-M Panthers, a D-I team. Because of their tough schedule, they had been struggling of late and had just suffered a big loss to Marquette, a perennial power and nationally ranked independent. We played the game downtown at the Milwaukee Arena, before a sparse crowd for such a large facility. Mike and Rex played sparingly. Jim was back to normal. The game was close for the first twelve minutes. They had some quick people in their backcourt who blew by us several times on fast breaks, to pull away to a 38-27 halftime lead. In the locker room we talked about tying up their defensive rebounders to delay their outlet passes and about sprinting back on defense. We went back out and fought back, much improving our transition defense, and shot a staggering 66% from the floor—our year's best half. No matter who was taking the shot that night, it seemed, he was eyeing a target as big as a bushel basket. With two minutes left, up 73-65, we went into "Melt," controlled the ball beautifully, and won 79-69. This was a huge victory for our program.

Back on the team bus, we were ready to celebrate. We scouted for a place to eat, and summoned Rex for a recommendation. Rex told Coach that he had a special place in mind and wanted to surprise us. "Coach—you need to trust me," he implored. "King, I trust you," Coach replied.

With that, Rex directed the driver. Soon a place with a familiar name appeared in the distance. When we arrived, we exited the bus and formed two lines. Coach climbed down the steps to a loud round of applause. He looked up to see the large marquee—LUBY'S CAFETERIA. "Welcome home, Coach," someone yelled. As he walked by, we all gave him high fives. Rex told the story to the manager, who discounted Coach's and our driver's meals. It was a wonderful night.

On February 14, 1989, we were slated to play a tough Stout team at home. Since this was Valentine's Day, we had a party planned at Joe's apartment after the game. We were all pumped, looking for a great night all around. We knew that Coach would suspect our plans, so we didn't bring our dress clothes along to the gym. The guys seemed a little chipper. When Coach arrived, we took our spots. The saying that night was:

TEAM DEFENSE CAN ONLY BE AS STRONG AS ITS WEAKEST INDIVIDUAL.

Coach, himself in a great mood, finished his pre-game speech early. He erased the board, scanned the room for a moment. Then from his pocket he extracted a marker and proceeded to draw a large heart on the board.

Coach explained that we would need to play this evening with great heart. He looked to the board, glanced back at us, turned again to the board, drew another heart, this one notably smaller. This heart symbolized Stout's heart. With that, he drew a lance piercing the smaller heart. Then he turned to us and said, "Lancers—let's break their hearts on Valentine's Day." The room erupted.

We took the floor. Amid an energetic warm-up, I spied

Terry and most of the team's dates sitting near Shirley, clad entirely in red. They were *all* in red, it appeared.

I looked to Joe, who had just retrieved a rebound. He glanced at me. "Red rum, red rum," he echoed.

The South 40, too, were in red, hands and faces painted as well. Our team really wanted to play well and get every player in the game. We got off to a great start. Everyone did play well, and we kept a comfortable lead the entire game, playing one of the better games in my memory. With two minutes to go, Coach called a timeout. We stood in one big huddle right on the court. He said, "Put your arms around each other and share this moment. You and your teammates have played a tremendous game." I'll never forget that public display of celebration exhibiting our unity and success. The final score was 104-82.

It was a jubilant locker room. We had a victory and a night to look forward to. Coach kept the post-game talk brief, capping it with, "Guys, have a great night. Be safe. And Joe—thank you in advance for watching out for everyone tonight."

Joe could only reply, "Yes, sir." It was obvious that Coach knew our plans.

In late February, 1989, our team was dealt a severe blow. We were in the locker room readying for our Wednesday practice. The day's saying read:

IT IS NOT ONLY A PRIVILEGE BUT
A RESPONSIBILITY TO BE ABLE TO

PLAY THE GAME OF BASKETBALL.

The Undertaker brought in a news item. His idol Alice Cooper had just announced he would run for governor of Arizona. Craig pinned the article next to Cooper's photo.

"This is amazing—truly amazing. In this country we can be whatever we want to be."

We laughed, and took the floor. I remember playing Horse with Rex. I was up H-O-R when I noticed Jim was not yet on the floor. This was unusual. He was one of the first of us here each day and usually played Pig with Chris and Andy.

Coach came into the gym. Solemnly he waved us to huddle up on the middle of the floor.

"Jim will not be here this evening," he announced. "I am sorry to report that his dad had a heart attack about noon today. He died very quickly. I'll have more information for you tomorrow. Please keep Jim and his family in your thoughts and prayers. If you want to stick around and shoot, fine. It's up to you. Coach Blank will be here. Our next practice will be tomorrow at 3:30."

This took a great deal out of our team. I don't think we ever recovered. Jim left the team and the Magnificent Seven that day. We attended the funeral and sat together behind his family. Jim's father had been one of our biggest boosters through the years. He never missed a home game during all those seasons. As for Jim, he didn't complete the school year nor did he graduate with our class. We all tried to stay in touch, but after about a month he got a job and continued to help at home with his family. As I look back, I wish there was something I could have done to be a better friend for him.

As our season got back into swing, it was all too obvious something was missing. It was hard to not think of Jim each day. The first game was at home against Lakeland College, with Joe scheduled to start in Jim's place. We decided to dedicate the season to Jim and his family and wore black wristbands on our left hands—the hands closest to our hearts.

We were in the middle of our warm-ups when I was summoned by the refs to come to mid-court to meet with the other captains. Always at that time Jim and I together would represent the team. As I walked towards half court I had a sinking feeling. I was alone, and I started to cry. I will never forget how each captain from Lakeland embraced me, gave me a long hug. They had heard what had happened, and their actions were truly a class act.

Before the game there was a moment of silence for Jim's dad. As play began, we seemed on cruise control and played lackluster. I couldn't wait for the game to end. With the crowd really behind us, we somehow got through, winning 74-65. To get that first game behind us was a real relief.

Each year we would hit the road for some exciting destination. This year was an exception—we would have two: Arizona and Florida. We had long looked forward to these trips. We were pumped.

On February 28, two coaches, fourteen players, and Ev landed in Flagstaff, Arizona. The Undertaker had hoped someway he would be able to see his idol Alice Cooper, who was thought to live in Paradise Valley, just west of Scottsdale. When we landed it was cold. Flagstaff is in higher country. The temperature was 48°, but the sun was beautiful and bright. We would play Northern Arizona University, the home of the Lumberjacks, that evening in their wooden dome.

We all walked around for half an hour to loosen up, then met for a shoot-around. Outside the dome, some of us took pictures next to a twenty-foot Lumberjack on display. Someone warned the freshmen to leave their pencils in their luggage. As we made our way down to the arena floor, we were greeted by a sign that read, "YOU ARE NOW AT 7,200 FEET ABOVE SEA LEVEL. EXERCISE WITH CAUTION." We assumed the sign was put there to intimidate opponents.

The dome was actually an indoor football stadium that doubled as a basketball arena. The large, expansive background beyond the baskets and the floor affected our depth perception and made for one great home-court advantage. NAU, in the Big Sky Conference, was a formidable D-I opponent.

After the short practice and pre-game meal, we rested in our motel rooms. A few hours later, we made our way to the dome to watch NAU's women's team defeat Grand

Canyon University. As we warmed up, we noticed few seats occupied in the ten-thousand-seat structure. Despite this, they had tradition, a loud band, and a truly unique way to introduce their team. They would start a chain saw and rev it each time a player's name was called. When the sound finally died down, we were ready to start.

The Lumberjacks were extremely tall and extremely talented. Their front line was 7'0", 6'10," and 6'9." Even Rex looked small. The Midget looked tiny. Joe said we should have had an inkling of this when we spotted the Lumberjack outside. We pressed, but NAU also had fine guards. We caused only six turnovers all night. We did play well, but their ability to grab offensive rebounds for second-chance points took its toll. Additionally, we knew that the sign at the top of the arena was there not just to warn us but to help us. Coach understood, and had been shuttling his players in and out of the game all game long. Out-rebounding us by eighteen, they beat us by a score of 85-69.

That night we had dinner at Black Bart's, a cowboy bar and restaurant where the servers are known to serenade their customers. We then went to bed early. Tomorrow would be a long day. Always making sure that wherever we traveled we could take advantage of any site-seeing opportunities, Coach had made special arrangements. After a quick breakfast we drove to the Grand Canyon—the first time that any of us, including the coaches, had ever seen this geographical wonder. To this day, it was the most awesome site I have ever seen. We walked and viewed for hours from different vantage points. Everyone took lots of pictures. Then we headed to Scottsdale by way of Sedona, a beautiful town of gorgeous red rocks and said to be located on several vortexes or energy fields. We had lunch overlooking a river at Slide Rock State Park. The main attraction was rock formations one could slide down or jump from into the river below. Coach made sure that we only remained observers.

By late afternoon we made it to Scottsdale, and had dinner. It was 89°. We were excited and spent the next hour resting beside the motel pool. Coach had instructed us; no one would swim on the day of a game. Meanwhile, Romeo dug up several contacts for a pool party later that night.

Then we got back to business. Southwest Bible College was a tiny NAIA school, but played efficiently. It was a very small gym, a crowd of perhaps 500. We were sluggish from the night before, but our talent and number of players made up for it. We won, 95-69, with everyone getting ample playing time.

Back at the motel we had a pizza party at the pool and were joined by some of Mike's newfound friends. We would meet them tomorrow as well. That night, for the first time, we heard a coyote howl. Crossing a street, we glimpsed a javelina, a wild pig. We never saw a rattlesnake, thank God!

Coach had reserved the next day for R&R, and we had a super time. The highlight was the Rainman's effort to perform a triple somersault in his pink-striped Speedo.

Meanwhile, Romeo got seven new phone numbers. Craig never did meet Alice Cooper.

COMING BACK FROM A LOSS IS ALL ABOUT CHARACTER

W e were home for only a short time—two games, wins over Ferris State and Minnesota-Duluth. On March 7, we traveled to Florida. On a layover in the Atlanta airport, we were lucky to bump into the Atlanta Hawks—Moses Malone, Dominique Wilkens, Reggie Theus, and, of course, Spud Webb. They were cordial and signed autographs as we stood beside as many as we could to physically compare ourselves. This team the Pistol himself had played for. I recall wishing he had been there. Dave was excited to see Spud and told him we had a play named after him. Joe told the Midget he finally found someone he could post up on.

We landed in Orlando on a beautiful, sunny day, loaded our vans, and drove to Deland, home of the Stetson Hatters. A very small, private school, Stetson was still a D-1 team. Our second-floor rooms at the Ramada Inn had balconies overlooking the campus—a beautiful setting with the many palm trees and fountains.

As Coach decided against a shoot-around, we opted for a tour. Making our way through the student union and out the far door, we ran into a cheerleading practice on the lawn. Romeo thought he had found the lost world. The girls had figured we were the opposing team, and came over to confirm it. Their captain, Angelita Carson, was a very pretty blonde, as was the entire squad. We talked and kidded. Romeo, of course, hit it off with Angelita. After about an hour we met the coaches for our team dinner. Then, after a short rest, we walked to the field house—a small building but very modern, seating about three thousand. They had a great band. The house was really rocking that night. It was their last home game of the year and it was Parents' Night.

As introductions came, Angelita's mom looked like an older sister; her dad seemed quite older. Next, the players— first our own. Not surprising, Romeo got a huge round of applause, and Angelita blew him kisses. Coach could only roll his eyes and shake his head.

With this, the lights went out. Immediately I thought of the Campbell game and the pelting eggs. A spotlight radiated in the middle of the floor: Each player jumped through a paper hoop reading "Crown them—Hatters!" as "Sweet Georgia Brown" played in the background. It was amazing, and got the crowd up.

The game began at a fast pace, with both teams not missing. We had trouble stopping them. Conversely, they couldn't stop our firepower. The size of the gym and the fine lighting seemed to make the basket larger. It was a seesaw game—the lead must have changed hands twenty times. Both teams made incredible shots, and the crowd responded with cheers and applause no matter which team scored. Romeo made three long three-pointers, and Angelita broke into a smile with each. I hit ten out of fourteen shots, one of my better games.

With eight seconds left and the score knotted at 96-96, Stetson possessed the ball. With our guards in a full-court press, the Midget turned his man twice before making a lunge. He caught a piece of the ball and deflected it toward the sideline, then gathered himself and dove through the air. Somehow he managed to flip the ball to the Undertaker, who was scurrying up from a help position. Craig grabbed the ball, took two hard dribbles, and tomahawked it through the basket.

The crowd was dumbstruck. We had beaten a D-I team on its own floor. In the locker room Coach was ecstatic, all smiles. In one corner stood the Midget, exhibiting a foot-long floor burn on one shin.

"Dave—was it worth it?" Coach asked.

"Every inch," Dave replied.

We dined near campus and were back in our rooms by 10:30 p.m. Within minutes word came out, we would get together with the Stetson cheerleaders. Only six of us—Rex, Mike, Dave, Joe, Craig, and I—sneaked out that night, the first and only time I ever left without permission from Coach. About 11 we snuck across the balcony past his room and down the stairs. I remember feeling it was a scene right out of "Hogan's Heroes." The sorority house wasn't difficult to find: We could hear the music blaring across the campus. The band from the game was playing. The place was jammed.

The cheerleaders made us feel very welcome. Everyone went wild. We danced and partied until 1:15 a.m., then pulled Romeo away and made our way back. One by one we stepped quietly back past Coach's room to our beds.

Seven a.m. came too quickly, but we knew we had to act as though we had gotten a full night's sleep. After a quick bite, we headed for Daytona Beach where, just the year before, Craig, Rex, Joe, Dave, Mike, and I had spent spring break. Taking turns driving on that trip, we had traveled straight through from school in Rex's dad's Suburban, very comfortable for six big guys. It had been a trip that everyone needs to take at least once, but we kept mum about it to Coach.

Approaching Nashville, we had been starving. Romeo had suggested a restaurant he had heard was a definite "ten." In this way, we had been introduced to Hooters, which Romeo had raved offered more than just a mite of "Southern hospitality." The skimpy outfits had led to a great time and a few jokes. Romeo had pronounced it the best establishment he had ever eaten at. Somehow we had known the menu had scarcely prompted that decision. Not surprisingly, we all had over-tipped.

The single Daytona motel room we all had shared was not on the beach and didn't even offer an ocean view. It was simply a room with two queen beds, sleeping quarters for the six of us. There were two to each bed, and Joe and I slept on futons on the floor. For the next six days, we had partied and tanned at poolside, made bonfires, gone swimming, and gotten little sleep. Except for Joe with his dark complexion, it hadn't taken us long to resemble lobsters.

Occupying the room next to ours had been four hilarious guys from Vanderbilt University, whom we had come to know well and do things with as a group. We had met students from all over the country, and some beautiful women. Romeo had been in his glory. Dave and I had barely noticed, since we had girlfriends, but the other guys had made up for us.

In Daytona, Coach took us to the famous Speedway. We examined the track and a few of the cars on display. Then it was off to the beach. Coach wanted us to see the Atlantic and put our feet in the water. As we walked and waded, we viewed last year's motel and reminisced about last year's spring break. It was like taking a trip—this time down Memory Lane.

Arriving in Tallahassee, home of Florida State University, our opponent for the evening, we were a bit sluggish. FSU was a big-time D-I opponent. We had our hands full. Their huge arena was packed. Their team was deep. We stayed close for the first twelve minutes, then they took control and steadily increased their lead. At halftime, Coach said we looked tired and needed to fight through it for twenty minutes more. He agreed that they were an extremely talented team—but added that this should only bring out the best in us. Rex, Craig and I each had three fouls. We must play *smarter*, Coach advised. "You must respect the game," he put it. "When you incur these fouls, you just can't aggressively take it to the hoop. You're dealt another hand."

The Seminoles were a class act. At halftime their staff brought in fresh towels, water, oranges, bananas, Coke, and Gatorade. We all felt like pros but wished that we had been playing at the same level. Whether it was their play or our sluggishness, I don't know. We lost 94-71.

After the game, Rick Sidler, an FSU student from Oconomowoc, Wisconsin, on a baseball scholarship, greeted me. We had played basketball against each other in high school. I remember him telling me how well I had played that night even though I had a season low twelve points.

The next morning we flew back. As we ducked back into our vans at the Milwaukee airport, snowflakes greeted us. We knew we were back in Wisconsin.

Tuesday, our final game of the year, would be at home. A victory would give us a number-one seed in the region, and Friday's and Saturday's playoff games would be on our home court, site of the South 40.

Everyone on campus was psyched. This was an all-important week for the team. My econ teacher, Professor Torrian, an enthusiastic fan who attended all our games, declared to the class that three vital events slated for March will have a huge effect on society: First, a major deal involving Ted Turner would merge Time and Warner to form Time-Warner. Second, our basketball team would earn a number-one seed for the national tournament. Third, the team would bring home the gold! The Professor, who had played at Marquette, was a close friend of Coach Lubinski. Once, he had given a fascinating lecture on basketball's own "supply and demand"—the supply of shots in a game and the demand for "good" shots.

Tuesday night might be the last time we would take the

floor at Lakefield. We wanted to make sure it wasn't. We went through our regular routine before the game. The saying on our board was:

OVER-CONFIDENCE ROBS A PLAYER
OF HIS MENTAL AND PHYSICAL
AGGRESSIVENESS.

Coach's pre-game talk was a great one focusing on being an aggressor and respecting our foe. We took the floor very focused, and played a near-flawless game against Michigan Tech with great confidence—only six turnovers—and winning 93-72. Five of us scored in double figures, led by Rex's twenty-three points and twelve rebounds. All the while the South 40 did its thing, and the crowd responded enthusiastically. We were ecstatic. Our victory had earned us the number-one seed for the D-II regional tournament. The second seed was Central Wisconsin, the third was Carroll, the fourth Kenosha-Parkside.

Friday night came in a flash. Central Wisconsin would play Carroll in the 5:45 game. Our game with Kenosha would follow.

Witnessing part of the first game was exciting. Both teams played at a high level. Just as the second half began, we took to the locker room to tape, dress, and become mentally prepared. The saying on the board was:

GREAT COMPETITORS DO NOT PERMIT
LITTLE THINGS TO BOTHER
THEIR PERFORMANCE.

Coach advised us: We must not let the crowd, the other

team, the refs—*anything*—compromise our concentration. We must simply remember "The sequence," and plug away. We soon got word: Central Wisconsin had defeated Carroll, 91-84. Central was a finalist. Our victory tonight would match us against them tomorrow .

Our game started out slowly. Neither team hit a high percentage. Despite Coach's timeouts to settle us down, Craig missed several easy inside shots. The Midget blew a lay-up. I was 0-5. The half found the score close, but we trailed, 26- 25. We made a couple of adjustments to our zone offense to put Craig on the high post to allow me to run the baseline. It worked. We scored the first ten points of the half and brought them out of their zone. It also built our confidence. Now we were all hitting our shots.

However, Kenosha heated up as well and nearly tied the score. With some four minutes left and the score 70-68, one of their players went to the line to attempt two free throws. En masse the South Forty stood up, turned around, and bent over—exposing their posteriors. Target signs hung on their rear ends. The rest of the crowd went wild with laughter. When the Parkside player missed his first attempt, the South 40 turned and bent again. Again he missed.

With three minutes to go and a 74-68 lead, we ran a successful "Melt" and hung on for a 79-76 victory. The King had 14 points and 10 rebounds. Craig had a game high 12 rebounds. I scored 17. Mike had 12. In the locker room, everyone talked about how the South 40 had influenced the game. We couldn't wait to see what they would come up with for the final!

Our record was 22-7. In a brief meeting after the game, we decided to discuss our plan for Central Wisconsin before tomorrow's game. We were slated to play at 7:30 p.m., with the winner earning a trip to the national tournament in Detroit. The game would be a repeat of an earlier meeting in November. There on their home court Central had won, 101- 93. Though their record was a respectable 24-5, our schedule had been stronger and our regional record better, landing us the number-one seed. This was so important—the ability to play at home. Meanwhile, all we had worked for those four years was on the line. We would arrive a little earlier than usual. Now we would go home and get *plenty of rest*.

On Saturday we met at the scheduled time. This time the saying was lengthier but just as profound:

TO SUCCEED, A TEAM MUST HAVE A SPIRIT OF COOPERATION, A GIVE-AND-TAKE ATTITUDE, A RESPECT FOR EACH OTHER'S ABILITY, AND A FEELING OF FRIENDLINESS AND HELPFULNESS BETWEEN PLAYERS AND COACH.

We went over several things they had done in our first meeting and what they had been up to of late. Like us, they were senior-laden, with ample experience and a very fine coach. I remember having a tough time running our sets against his switching defense. We would make several adjustments. We would run some counters and pressure releases to stop their aggressiveness. Coach summarized: "To succeed tonight we will have to meet the challenge head on. No matter what happens, good or bad, we must accept it and keep playing. All of us have been through this before. We must listen to each other, *help* each other, *play through* any issues."

We took the floor for our final Lakefield warm-up. The crowd was a huge one. The place rocked. Our band was playing energetically. The South 40 were all decked out—this time in farmer outfits, with a bale of hay propped up in one corner. Conspicuous in front, Koo Koo was organizing like a maestro leading his orchestra—now sending boos out at the other teams warm-up shots. Parents were there. Professor Torrian even gave extra credit for attendance. The cheerleaders were in full force, led by Midge. Painted signs for luck showed all over the gym, complements of Professor Febrantz, Sam Evans, and the art students. Masahisa Amano wore a martial-arts outfit. He would be ready for anything. Again and again the "Wave" went around the gym, causing Shirley to rise and grin each time with zest. I even glimpsed Trevino, high in the stands.

Yes, Lakefield was there in full force. We would play a game never to forget. The buzzer sounded. Introductions came. I got visible goose bumps as I heard my name for the last time.

The game started out very physically—six fouls in the first two minutes. The refs were going to keep things under control, and as we had been taught, we adjusted to their lead.

Both teams moved the ball well, and players were working hard on defense to minimize uncontested shots. Each team wanted to fast break, but the hustling transition defenses eliminated any fast-break opportunities. As a result, the game was somewhat low scoring. Each team had to secure opportunities through its patterned offense.

With thirty seconds left in the half, the score 33-33, Joe's three-pointer bounced long off the rim. Central's two man grabbed the ball at about the foul line, and raced down the court. The Midget sprinted off. As the Central player went up for the dunk, Dave dove high into the air and slapped the ball off his leg. The ref motioned: Lakefield's ball. The place went crazy! Dave had ended up rolling into the stands of the South 40. As the ref was signaling, Koo Koo and two other farmers were picking Dave up and patting him on the butt and pushing him back onto the court. As Dave positioned himself to take the ball out of bounds, I noticed he had several pieces of hay in his hair.

With ten seconds left, we ran "Double." I came off a staggered double pick, found myself open, and hit a three. The crowd erupted. We ran off the floor.

We were up 36-33 and halfway to Detroit. In the locker room we could hear all the festivities going on outside. Coach was concerned about our fouls. Four of us had three; three of us had two. "The particular situation is this," he put it. "We must learn to play smarter, stay out of bad situations. We must contest all shots, but we don't have to block them. Show the refs that you're putting your hands straight up, that there is no contact. Keep moving your feet on defense. Stay in front of your man. And, above all, give them one and *only* one opportunity. Fellas—*no* second chance points."

We came determined to take our game to another level, but Central had other ideas. The contest became a dogfight. As the minutes went along, every possession became more critical. Amid extremely physical play, each team lost two players. We lost Joe and David. Several others, including Rex and me, had four fouls.

With four minutes left we were up by six—only to have Central tie us with two long-range threes. "It all comes down to execution," Coach harped as we raced by. He was exactly right. We had been scouted well. Central had answers for many of our sets. Leading 88-87, with a minute and two seconds to go, Central came down the court with what would be their last possession. "Lancer, Lancer, Lancer!" Coach yelled, to get us to step up and meet the challenge. The crowd was standing, shrieking and cheering us on. The noise level was sky high. Despite, oddly, I could still hear the squeaks of sneakers as we fought through screens to cut off and impede their progress. We kept the ball out of the paint, protecting the castle.

With twenty-two seconds left, in an effort to beat the shot clock they hoisted a three-pointer from the right wing. It bounced high and was snagged by Mike, who had put a picture-perfect block on his man on the opposite elbow. We had held our ground and come up with a huge stop.

The outlet pass went to the Midget, who quickly brought

the ball across half-court. Then he coiled up with the ball, securing it with two hands, looked to the ref, and yelled for a timeout. We had 12.4 seconds left to secure a victory.

As we huddled, Coach took a long, deep sigh, then explained. His voice exuded confidence as he spoke, "To inbound the ball securely, we will run SOB number two. If they are in a 1-3-1, we'll go to our box set, penetrate to get to the hole, and, if necessary, kick the ball back out for a J. Since we don't need a three, we must move in to midrange and look for open spaces. If they are in a two-guard zone, we'll run Gap Movement, look to the short corner, hit the gaps, and swing the ball. Finally, if they are in man we'll run our bread and butter—Go-5—so be sure to get to your spots and trust each other." Then he said, "Guys, I can guarantee they'll be in a man-to-man. Just inbound the ball and read the defense."

We all clasped hands for the final time, and called "One, two, three—*finish!*"

As we ran the out-of-bounds play, the Midget secured possession in the back court. Central was in a 1-3-1 defense, hands high. As Dave brought the ball across half-court, their coach yelled "Now!" and quickly they shifted into a man-to-man. Coach had guessed correctly. Dave surveyed the court and gave us time to assume our spots. The alignment left him at the top of the key, the King on the right elbow, Craig on the left, I on the block below the King, and Romeo on the block below Craig—a box set. With eight seconds left, Dave stutter-dribbled, yelled, "Go!", and dribbled to the right wing. I would wait one count and then angle up to back-pick Craig's man on the left elbow. The Undertaker would spin and cut to the low block I had vacated, and Dave would have a good look at him. After setting this back screen, The King would come over and join me to set a staggered double screen for Romeo, who would curl around towards Dave for a free-throw-line jumper. We had practiced this play at least three times a week all year and had run it several times. Each time it had paid off.

I made my move, set a solid back pick. Craig spun, and moved to the low block. There he spread his legs and elbows out and kept his hands high in a ready position, like a catcher anticipating a game-winning fastball. Rex and I made our way to set the double screen. With the screen in place, Mike jab-stepped toward the middle, then curled around the wall we had set and headed for the free throw area. This afforded the Midget two options, with the higher-percentage shot being from an inside pass to Craig. Dave made the inside pass, using deception. His defender was 6'4'. He was 5'8". Coach had taught us to make a clean entry pass, we had to fake a pass, then make a pass. As Dave passed, his taller defender caught a piece of the ball, which sailed slowly toward Craig like a lame duck. To prevent anyone else from gaining possession, Craig rushed a few steps forward to secure the ball, but vacated his great low-post position. Our post people had been taught—possession first, position second. This left Craig with the ball some ten feet from the basket with 5.2 seconds left, with our team still down 88-87.

To give him room, prevent the double-team, and allow the second option, Dave cut to the corner, taking his defensive man along. Now the Undertaker sought the second option—Mike at the free throw area. Normally, the pass would have come from Dave. Now it was up to Craig. However, the tipped pass had given Mike's defensive man time enough to catch up to him. Mike was completely covered.

The Undertaker squared up, pump-faked, then drove toward the basket on the baseline side. The Midget's defensive man slid in to provide help. Craig could only jump-stop and fan the ball back to Dave in the corner. With 1.3 seconds left, the Midget hoisted a rainbow jumper over his defender—the last shot to be taken by the Magnificent Seven at Lakefield. The ball hit the rim, bounced high. We pounded the boards in an effort to tip the ball in. In their haste, both Craig and Rex knocked down their opponents. The rest of us got tangled in the lane. Bodies were everywhere. The only ones still standing were Dave and his defender, in the corner. The horn sounded. Had I missed a whistle?

I looked up—and saw the refs heading off the court. I stood up slowly, realizing our careers were over.

We lined up and congratulated Central. They had played well, had kept us from executing. They deserved the victory.

In a locker room filled with tears, Coach made his final speech. He thanked us for our efforts. He never pointed the finger at anyone. He never mentioned our last possession. Instead, he told us we were a very special group, a group he would never forget. "I love you guys," he said, finally, and went around the room to shake everyone's hand.

The team assembled two days later to turn in gear and take care of paperwork. The message on the board that day was:

I WANT TO THANK ALL OF YOU FOR YOUR EFFORTS AND PLAYING FOR LAKEFIELD. IT WILL BE MY PLEASURE TO HELP PLACE MY PLAYERS IN GOOD JOBS UPON THEIR GRADUATION. MY DUTY DOESN'T END AFTER GRADUATION OR THAT FIRST JOB. CONTACT WITH FORMER PLAYERS IS IMPORTANT, AND I STAND READY AND EAGER TO HELP THEM ADVANCE IN THEIR CHOSEN PROFESSIONS.

I stared at the message for a long time. Then I turned in my gear, filled out the paperwork, and left.

TEN

OF ALL THE THINGS YOU WEAR, YOUR EXPRESSION IS THE MOST IMPORTANT

For the next few weeks, it was very difficult to think about life without basketball. I could coach, sure, but playing for Luby with that goal of a national championship—that was gone forever. Even the campus was subdued. Professor Torrian didn't talk basketball. Like most of the guys, I was somewhat depressed by this disaster. We had not yet come to terms with the finality of our basketball careers. I guess we just needed more time.

Central went on to finish third nationally. In my business class the big story was the *Exxon Valdez* oil spill, another disaster. Some 10.8 million gallons—240,000 barrels—of unrefined Alaskan crude had poured into Prince William Sound in one of the worse man-made environmental disasters ever.

In April, Michigan defeated Seton Hall 80-79 to win the NCAA national title. The Wolverine's Glenn Rice was named tournament MVP.

Graduation was always an awesome occasion at Lakefield. This year's was no exception. All our parents and friends attended. Our group–Mike, Rex, Joe, Craig, Dave and I—sat together, along with Terry, who by now was a regular. The college's president, professors, and staff honored us and welcomed us. We would be members of the Lakefield family forever. Our valedictorian, Midge Rennicke, stressed our responsibility to move forward with distinction and class and make this a better world for all. She advised, "Lead with your smile. This projects an atmosphere of trust and love in the world."

Our featured speaker, astronaut Jim Lovell, had flown two Gemini flights and missions in Apollo 8 and Apollo 13. With his son at St John's Military Academy in Delafield, it was convenient for Mr. Lovell to address us.

He read very special and appropriate lines, from Chris Rea's song "Heaven":

Caught in the void and empty space
In between there and back
And the paradise of going somewhere
That's still so far away
Happy, boy, you bet I am!
Holding on to this smile
For just as long as I can.
Heaven—It's all bright in front
And it's all dark behind
Livin' for the now that's
In between the bridges and the signs
And getting there is still
A long way to go.

The president finally uttered those magic words, "Ladies and gentlemen, I now present to you the class of 1989."

We threw our flat, tasseled hats in the air. Trevino came by with high-fives and congratulations. Coach and Shirley gave each of us a touching, handwritten card and a long, special hug.

We promised each other that we would stay in touch, close touch. We would be there for each other. Always.

ELEVEN

SUCCESS IS MORE ATTITUDE THAN APTITUDE

L ooking back, I realize that what has fascinated me most through the years is Luby's coaching style. In 1996, I decided to earn my Master's in sports management at the United States Sports Academy. My thesis, "Coaching Leadership Style as a Predictor of Team Success in High-School-Varsity Boy's Basketball in the State of Wisconsin," sought to define the mentoring that would most often breed success. My data encompassed not only coaches but players. I had both groups fill out questionnaires and provide records. I felt that, since many players desired to participate in the team's decision-making processes which influenced their performances and satisfaction, perceptions of athletes also were important. Any player's perception of his coach's leadership style influences team success. My findings defined four alternatives:

1. **Autocratic**: The coach makes all decisions based on information at hand.

2. **Consultive**: The coach shares problems, solicits suggestions, and then makes decisions.

3. **Participative**: Team members decide jointly with the coach, who is just another member.

4. **Delegative**: The coach delegates decisions to the players and abides by their decisions.

From my own coaching experience, I knew that many mentors used styles with which they were comfortable or which they had copied from others whom they considered as role models to guide teams. Some coaches chose styles that worked best for them; others were willing to alter their styles to improve their win-loss records.

I found the inquiry fascinating and learned a great deal. Many coaches used the authoritarian style simply because they thought a coach was an authority figure. Some had a need for control, and coaching met that need. Also, stressful situations added to the need to control team members. Teams under stress *preferred* a take-charge person. Finally, many less-confident players, to feel more comfortable, needed a coach who was a dominant figure.

Conversely, democratic styles such as players calling their own plays and determining lineups by team votes were options. These styles intimated that coaches were more approachable, which resulted in better communication and improve a coach's ability to learn athletes' fears or dissatisfactions that could hurt a team. Also, more independent players would perhaps better handle stressful situations.

In all, I concluded that the style most effective in achieving success in high-school basketball was—the authoritarian.

My study also revealed that the style employed was definitely affected by pressure on a coach to win. Yet, at Lakefield (a college setting—plenty of pressure to win), Luby never let it be known to us that he was under so much pressure. He would openly say, "When we walk out of Lakefield, we must leave behind our four years of striving to become the best possible players we could be. Wins? Wins would follow accordingly."

In hindsight, I see how much his philosophy worked to

self-motivate us. The administration seemed pleased with Luby and the program. Administration, teachers, and Luby called us "student-athletes." Coach would also say that, if each of us were to look at his total college experience and subtract basketball from that sum (yes, another math equation), he would settle for nothing less than an experience as enriching and gratifying as any other student's.

Although my study included a high-school atmosphere and population, I feel confident that I can link its findings to my years coached by Luby. While he for the most part used an authoritarian style, he did allow players to decide on team travel, captains, play suggestions, warm-ups, and the like. Why? I believe that the maturity level of our team was a factor. During my Lakefield career, it seemed that Coach's style eased from strict authoritarianism. The key was—building trust.

If I had to define it, I would say that Coach combined the authoritarian and consulting styles. But the real beauty was—he knew exactly when to utilize each one. This led to our players' cohesiveness and ability to get along so well. In my day I have experienced coaches who are overly authoritarian and volatile. As players more often develop personalities that directly reflect their coach, they will inherit, as if by osmosis, many of his traits. Overbearing, up-down-personality coaches create players with similar characteristics. Their teams have many highs and lows. They may be able to beat a formidable opponent one night or lose to a mediocre one the next. By contrast, Luby coached on an even keel, counseling us to wear the same game face always, regardless of the peaks and valleys.

To me, basketball has always meant so very much. It is an aesthetic, exciting game that demands physical skills as well as mental toughness. Played correctly, it is the ultimate team game. Former UCLA coach John Wooden put it well: The most important quality a player can have is "controlled quickness." If this is true, the ability to bring out the best in your teammates cannot be far behind. The most recent example has to be Phoenix Sun Steve Nash. Nash embodies teamwork and team spirit every time he takes the floor, eliciting the maximum from each of his teammates. Many other players in the league wish they could take the floor with Steve. When the NBA named Nash the MVP in 2006, they got it right.

I could have gone on, but had I daydreamed more, I would have been late for or missed my first class. That night I called each of my former teammates and made contact with everyone but Mike. It was great to reminisce. Rex the King had been married for only six months and was now divorced. He was using his accounting degree as a controller for a packaging company in Green Bay. Rainman Joe was married and had two children, a boy and a girl (just like Terry and I). Terry and I had attended Joe's daughter's confirmation about two years ago. The reception had been at Peppies, which Joe now owned and managed. His son Joe, Jr., was working for him as a busboy, and the family lived in West Allis. Dave the Midget had married, divorced, and remarried. With three boys from his first marriage, he was now wed to a Korean woman. Recently he had changed his job, but he was still selling pharmaceuticals. And, no, he hadn't pursued the comedian career that seemed so appropriate. Craig the Undertaker had been working for Andrews's Rest In Peace Mortuary as— yes—a mortician for the last eighteen years. He was married, had a daughter, and lived in Madison. Jim, married and living in Nashota, had a daughter Becky, who was seventeen, and a son Bill, who was eight. Jim, bartending at Lake Shore Country Club, had never finished school. About three years ago we golfed together at Nagawaukee. He beat me again.

Most importantly, each of the guys remembered our days together with fondness and thought that a reunion was in order.

Late the next evening I got a return call from Romeo Mike. He was working as a TV anchor in Dubuque, Iowa. His shift didn't finish until 11 p.m. Divorced, Mike confided that he didn't have any children, but wished he did. He, too, hoped for a get-together in the near future. He suggested a three-day Las Vegas weekend.

Some days later I took the bull by the horns and sent an email chain offering three possibilities for us to meet in Las Vegas. Everyone liked the site. The difficulty was to find a suitable date for everyone. Within three weeks, however, the details were worked out. We decided to meet on April 13. Four of us—Dave, Joe, Jim, and I—would arrive together. Rex, Mike, and Craig would come in on other flights. We decided to get four rooms—Rex and Craig in one, Joe and Dave in another, Jim and I in the third, and Mike in the fourth. Asked if he minded rooming alone, Mike showed himself to be the same old Romeo. "No," he replied. "It probably won't be for long!!"

Excitement was building. Crazy emails and phone calls flew back and forth. We were all eagerly anticipating our reunion and planned to meet in the Luxor lobby on Friday at 5 p.m. Joe asked, "Why the pyramid-shaped hotel? Because it is reminiscient of a hierarchy of needs?" Rex eagerly offered to pick the restaurants for the "roadtrip." Mike looked forward to the palm trees and bikini weather. Craig emailed (and, of course, sent copies to all of us) telling the Midget, "Don't expect to find a small, small world in Vegas. But we will keep an eye out for Mickey Rooney!" Rainman? Rainman put it this way, "Joe Sorelli like numbers. Joe Sorelli like numbers. Who's on first?"

TWELVE

SUCCESS COMES IN CANS—
FAILURE COMES IN CAN'TS

I could hardly wait for the 14th. Terry was very excited for me and told me to give the guys her very best. I told her—she should come. Wasn't she an integral part of our group? But no. "It's a guy thing," she emphasized.

I took the day off from school and managed a leisurely ride to the airport. Dave, Joe, and Jim were already there. Within a short time the flight was announced, and we were on our way. In no time we were landing. Viva, Las Vegas! We took a cab to the Luxor, an impressive building shaped into a thirty-story pyramid. We checked in and agreed to meet in the lobby at 3 p.m. to explore the hotel before the others arrived. At 4:50 p.m. we eagerly waited in the lobby. Within minutes Rex, Mike, and Craig emerged from the crowd.

More than eighteen years had passed, but the Magnificent Seven were now together again. It was incredible to see everyone and how affectionately we all still kidded one another. We had a bellhop take several pictures of our group. Extremely hungry, we decided on the closest restaurant in the hotel and ordered drinks in the bar while we waited for our table.

We took turns updating the years since graduation. I began by telling about my teaching and coaching job at Pewaukee High School. Everyone was amazed that I had already been a head coach for twelve years. My kids, Kim and Adam, were fourteen and ten. Kim loved volleyball. Adam was going to be the next Steve Nash. Terry loved her nursing job. Our three-bedroom home, while not on a lake like I had always hoped, was cozy. We loved it. We were lucky to have each other and our security. "Terry sends everyone her very best!" I told the group.

Craig was next. He had been married to Melissa for nine years. Their daughter Abbey had just turned eight. She loved to dance and was in her fourth year at the Pixie Dance Studio. Since he had left school, Craig had been working at the mortuary, and was now the manager and about to purchase the business. Dave was swift to interject—"I'll bet people are dying to be *your* customers!!" Craig laughed. "I know it sounds like a dark, depressing occupation," he conceded, "but we've helped many families in their time of direst need. Melissa works with me in the office. Living in Madison, we frequently attend Wisconsin Badger basketball games."

Rex had been married to Cindy Strauss from Green Bay for only six months. She had graduated from Lakefield the year after we did. He had hoped things would work out, but unfortunately they didn't. His divorce had been finalized four years ago. He had no children. He had passed the C.P.A. exam when he was twenty-eight and now had worked for three years as a controller for Green Bay Packaging, a corrugated container plant. Rex had recently bought a condo on the Fox River, and said he could walk a short block to one of the best fishing spots in the state. He had attended three Packer games last year and simply loved Lambeau Field. He emphasized that he had no refrigerator in his office. We knew better!

Dave had divorced Ann, who had also graduated with our class. Their three boys John, Mark, and Michael were seventeen, fourteen, and twelve. Now wed to a Korean woman named Lolee and living in Hartland, Dave had recently changed jobs, but was still selling pharmaceuticals. His boys were all involved in basketball, and he had helped coach their teams. Dave and Lolee had recently bought a new home on the edge of the city and he had just taken up golf— but he would be making no wagers with Jim in the near future.

Joe reported that life was good. He and his wife Monica had been married for sixteen years and had two children, Joe, a fourteen-year-old high-school freshman, and Stacey, nine. He owned and managed Peppies, an Italian restaurant, and Monica helped as well. Joe, Jr., following in his footsteps, was already bussing tables. He was also interested in competitive swimming and on the school team. Stacey wanted to be the next "American Idol." He added that, although it was great for all of us to get away, the next time would be a big dinner in his private room at Peppies.

Jim told us about his wife Eleanor and how lucky he was. They had been married for eighteen years, with a daughter Becky, seventeen, and a son Bill, eight. Becky was a senior at Oconomowoc High School and planned to major in nursing at UW-Madison. With her interest in golf and their house near the first fairway of Pagonnica Golf Course, Jim enjoyed giving Becky lessons. Eleanor was working for American Family Insurance and Jim as head bartender at the country club. He regrets not having his degree, he reported, but his work hours gave him enough time to play eighteen holes almost whenever he wanted. He had considered a management job a few years back. Now he was considering a run for mayor.

Finally, there was Mike, an anchorman in Dubuque. Having been married to Sarah, a TV reporter, for two years and to Ashley, a news producer, for three, he was currently single, with no kids. He was still hoping to make it big time in New York. He owned a condo and was considering getting a cat. He hoped someday to have a family.

During dinner we reminisced about the good old days, about former students and teachers and their current whereabouts. Coach had retired twelve years earlier. At his request, Lakefield did not have a ceremony. The program was not about him, he felt. It was about the many student athletes who had taken the floor. I had kept in touch, and he had sent me all his basketball books, tapes and materials— which I felt honored to have in my possession. Coach Blank had moved on to the University of Wisconsin-Whitewater as a phy-ed teacher. Professor Torrian was now teaching at the School of Business at Marquette University. Koo Koo Kramer? We concluded he must be working as a bouncer somewhere. And Ev? By now he must be Bill Gates's right-hand man!

After dinner we strolled to another hotel. The lights of the city were brilliant against the night sky. You could easily see how Las Vegas had been coined "the city that never sleeps." We had reservations for the House of Blues concert at the nearby Mandalay Bay at 9 p.m. The show was incredible, very entertaining. As we headed back for some sleep—except for Mike, who decided to check out the Mandalay Bay bar—we all decided on a late breakfast, at about 10:30 in the morning.

The next day was beautiful and sunny, not a cloud in the sky. At the buffet we ate like kings and kidded about staying for the rest of our lives. As we were eating, two attractive women strutted past our table on the way to the pool. "Good morning, Mikey!!" they called. We laughed. "Mikey?" we repeated. Mike seemed embarrassed. He had met them in the bar the night before and had talked to them for several hours, he explained.

After breakfast we headed to the pool. The complex was gorgeous, with palms lining the area, a waterfall in the middle, and a huge jacuzzi in the corner that must have seated twenty-five. For the rest of the day we tanned, swam, and sat around. We had drinks and snacks delivered and reminisced, talked and laughed all day. At about 3 p.m. we decided on a game of water volleyball and took on a group of guys from Intel here for a week of training. The Magnificent Seven was back in full force. It was great to see our competitive side again. We won easily, and at times showed compassion for our less athletic opponents. As we readied to leave for dinner, we noticed Mike—the sole guy in the Jacuzzi, with what appeared to be fifteen women! Rex, our self-appointed photographer, sneaked over to snap a photo of the group.

That evening we had reservations at the Strip Steak. We decided on the theme for the night. Each one of us would have to tell in detail his absolute favorite "Luby" story. In addition, everyone had to wear a Hawaiian or tropical shirt. This, too, would be in honor of Coach Lubinski. Hadn't he told us he would take our team to Hawaii for a tournament our senior year but could never swing it?

We met in the lobby—an array of the most colorful shirts you could imagine, drawing double-takes from passers-by. We had our picture taken by the concierge as a memento. As we filed out, we spied a group of Japanese snapping a photo of a sculpture in the lobby. Rex got an idea: He would take *their* photo. The photo was a classic. Japanese tourists intently taking pictures with *their* cameras.

At the Strip Steak, our alcove table lent us the opportunity for a near-private dinner. The waitress was outstanding and very personable. She took our drink orders and returned in a flash. To celebrate the occasion, we all ordered drinks with tiny umbrellas protruding. Joe gave a fine, heartfelt toast to the Magnificent Seven and to Luby. He deeply appreciated that we had all taken time from our busy schedules to do this. We then decided we would each tell our unique Luby story over desert. The steaks were incredible. Rex's was by far the largest. He had ordered the forty-two ouncer—which looked like a large roast on his plate. Craig quipped, "It's obvious Rex isn't a vegetarian!!"

As we finished, I called for order and announced: It was time to tell the stories. We all prepared to hear some crazy, wacky tales embellished to the point of absurdity. However, this night the words spoken by my teammates would prove to be ones I would never forget.

I began, with the premise that I would tell the story that I remember the most about Coach Luby.

When I was in college, I was worried—really worried—about my future. My family didn't have a lot of money. To me, receiving a scholarship was no less than incredible, like winning the lottery. I wanted to make sure I made the best of it. Dad had worked for a company for over twenty-seven years which had been bought out by a larger firm. My senior year of high school, Dad lost his job and upcoming pension as well. With no degree, he had to resort to manual labor, taking jobs far beneath his abilities. The money I made in the summer was needed for the family. As a result, even though I really had an interest in business, there was a sour taste in my mouth about corporate America, and employee vulnerability. I thought that my degree might end up as a piece of paper I would never use and feared that I, too, might end up without any control over my life.

Though we really never discussed it to any great length, Coach seemed to understand my fears. He always told me things would work out if I maintained a positive attitude and moved forward. Doors would open up that I never thought were available. Was I getting an early indoctrination in someone moving my cheese, as in Spencer Johnson's popular book *Who Moved My Cheese*? When he came to me at the end of the first semester in my sophomore year and pitched his business-education idea, I was elated. I had a propensity for business, yes, and I truly loved basketball. Now I could have both, a quality life unequaled any other way. He also told me not once but several times that I was very lucky to have Terry, that we were a great combination that could help many other people.

Dave then asked me, "Back in college you would always say, 'I've got that feeling.' What *was* that all about?"

A bit embarrassed, I replied, "When I was young, on game days and sometimes even days before, I would get this feeling. It would take over me. The anticipation of the competition. I think everyone gets this type of feeling to some degree and can personally relate to it. For me, it was a feeling that I cherished and loved. When we played our last game at Lakefield, I was sad. I thought that I would never get this feeling again, a feeling I so loved. Well, I got into coaching and—lo and behold!—the feeling was there. Yes, the same feeling came over me. I was elated. Coach taught us that by giving of ourselves we would receive even greater gifts. I certainly did."

This said, I turned to Mike, sitting on my left.

Mike, forever our rah-rah guy, now had an unusual aura about him, different from anything we'd ever seen before. He started off, "If it hadn't been for Coach, I would never have graduated. My major required a science course. I was convinced there was no way I could pass. I absolutely *hated* science, had no aptitude for it, no confidence in my ability to learn it. I even considered changing my major—or even transferring. After several lengthy discussions with Coach and not-so-accidentally bumping into his wife Shirley, I agreed that I would give it a try. They told me to have confidence in my abilities and work hard and the results would be positive," he recounted. "Shirley tutored me six hours per week for the entire semester while I took the course. Amazingly—*amazingly*—I got a C. I so appreciated what they both did for me, but I've always felt guilty. The semester they helped me was the second semester of our senior year—my last. When we were at Stetson and snuck out, I couldn't help but think of all they had invested in me. For me to treat them this way? I guess my hormones just took over that night."

Several of us replied in unison, "*That* night?"

Jim was next. He told us that when his dad died he was totally distraught. Coach had been the one who came and got him from class. "He took me to the hospital and was there with me when he died. You remember all that Coach did at the wake and funeral? That wasn't all. He and Shirley had me over once every week for dinner. We talked for hours—even though I wasn't on the team. Coach said that I would always be part of the team and the Lakefield family. I had been on a half scholarship and I had some loans outstanding. He offered to help me to get through the semester financially. I resisted. I pushed away and took the job at a country club that would help my family at the moment but screw up my future. Though I didn't take his suggestion, Coach still supported me and my decision. Later that year he gave me my sports letter and an award for courage—even though I was not technically on the team. He and Shirley wanted me to get my degree. They always emphasized the importance of education. In hindsight, yes, I should have listened."

Then it was Dave's turn. "Coach had been there for the worst period of my life. My junior year at Lakefield, my parents planned to divorce, and separated. I was really down. It was eating me alive. Coach and I would talk about it for hours. He counseled me, and convinced me that the situation had nothing to do with *me*. It wasn't *my* fault. Coach talked to Mom and Dad individually, even attended family counseling with them and me. During the sessions he was incredible. I'll never forget when he said—'It had to be a very strong love that produced such a wonderful young man.' That, I think, was the major turning point. My parents became more committed right then and there. They worked together to save their marriage and keep our family intact. Coach *believed* in family. After all—weren't we all a family at school?"

He turned. Rex nodded, and began. All his life he had had a serious weight problem. "You know how I love my food. Through the years it has been the source of many jokes, but it was— and is—a serious disorder. When I arrived at Lakefield as a freshman, Coach had issues with my weight. He made me agree to maintain a certain weight for the season and kept a tight watch on me in the off-season. He even had me join Overeaters Anonymous and attend a monthly session I never once had to pay for. He put me in charge of picking out dining spots as a reward for my diligence. If Coach hadn't taken control, I would have had a major issue competing in basketball at the college level. Occasionally he would tell me, 'You are what you eat'—and hand me a piece of fruit. When he gave us the Christmas baskets with the fruit and candy each year, my contents were a bit different than yours. Mine contained healthy snacks along with a note congratulating me on my will power. Even today, when I want to binge, I somehow always think of Coach and find the courage to fight the desire."

"Did you find that same courage with your steak tonight?" jabbed the Midget. Rex smiled and nodded.

"Actually I did. I had been seriously considering the fifty-six-ouncer."

Joe hesitated for a second, then began. "You guys always kidded me about having Mafia ties? Well let me tell you how relieved I was when you nicknamed me 'Rainman' and dropped the Mafia moniker. My grandfather was in the Mafia, and taught me first hand about gambling. For me, it was poker and at age seventeen, I was addicted to the game and losing a lot of money. When I arrived at Lakefield I had a problem—a huge problem and owed about $4,000 in gambling debt. It was a good thing, at least for me, that we didn't have control of our scholarship money. I'll never know how, but Coach detected my problem. Coach called me to his office and sat me down. It was that day in his office that I came to realize, and finally *admitted*, 'I am an addict!' I agreed to counseling to overcome my addiction and promised Coach, then and there, that I would NEVER gamble again. A promise is a promise. Coach sent me to a great counselor who recommended that I also attend 'Gamblers Anonymous.' The counseling also included money management classes, and my counselor worked with me to set up a payment plan and found me a great summer job. With the money I earned during the summers, I was able to maintain my payment schedule. When I graduated, I was debt-free, which I owe all to Coach. I never forgot the desperation I felt about this addiction and how Coach freed me from it. I could *never* have gone to my dad. Coach made me keep my promise—not for him but for myself."

It was Craig's turn. He looked down, hesitated, then looked to the group. "My … Luby story is really hard to tell," he said. "Since all of you have been so open, I'll be, too. I have always been a little different from most. I never put two and two together. You know how I was very introverted and dressed so different? Coach talked to me several times. He knew there were issues. He teamed me up with a school psychologist who referred me to a counselor. The sessions were pricey but I didn't pay a dime. I'm not sure what coach did to work that out. Why? My stepdad abused me as a kid. My folks split when I was thirteen. Stepdad's now in prison. The result—I could cope much better. My self-esteem shot up. Remember all the rules Coach had about dress and appearance but always seemed to let me off the hook? Well, he thought it was more important for me to feel accepted than maintain his dress code. Coach gave up some of what he believed in to help me be part of the team. He thought of the team first more than anyone I'll ever know. Truly—he was my savior."

We all sat by, astonished, pensive, and silent. We had anticipated a night of Luby stories such as the Henway or the famous leap. We'd be rolling on the floor, we thought, crying as we laughed. Instead, our stories had turned out like episodes of Dr. Phil. Each of us had never known our team-mates' issues. My issue—what would I do with my degree? This seemed so petty compared to the problems of my buddies. All these years, each of us had thought he had been the only one with a problem.

A new understanding had dawned—and a far greater respect for what we had accomplished. The common denominator overcoming all these obstacles? Coach. Apparently he hadn't worked just to coach basketball and teach math. In light of these real-life issues, his day jobs had been minor. We had each been a work in progress that he had made it his duty to turn into a finished product.

We finished dessert. The waitress brought the check. Dave looked to Joe.

"So I guess the choice of Vegas wasn't a great idea for you?"

Everyone chuckled. Joe looked to Dave. "Actually it was," he said.

Rex jumped in quickly. "Remember, guys—what happens in Vegas, stays in Vegas!"

With four of us scheduled to fly out in the early afternoon, we decided to meet at 8:30 a.m. for breakfast. It had been a great weekend, one none of us would forget. Since this would be our last time together until who-knew-when, we were all notably quiet, even subdued.

At the table Dave was thumbing through the *Las Vegas Sun*. Suddenly he exclaimed, "Oh, my God!!"

We could tell by his excitement that he had an idea.

"Guys—check this out!"

He flashed us a large ad, for a forty-and-over basketball tournament, a national tournament that would allow ninety teams to enter. According to the ad, it was extremely competitive. Participants in the past had included many ex-college and pro athletes. A Las Vegas team, the High Flyers, had won it all the last two years.

Dave peeked down and gawked. "And you will not believe where it's being held—the Stetson University campus!"

We laughed. "We've never lost there," said Joe. "I *love* that place," put in Romeo. "I've never been there, but I wish I could have been," added Jim. "You guys *serious*?" asked Rex.

We looked around. An idea—*the* idea—was taking shape. All at once everyone was nodding, jabbering. Excitement hung in everyone's voice.

Dave went on. Sponsored by the City of Deland, the tournament called for an entry fee of $500—and a winner's prize of $10,000. Games would start July 5 and run for five consecutive days.

I formed my hands into a timeout sign and drew a laugh from everyone.

"If we are going to do this, we have to be serious. We need to be in shape, arrive early, and *all* of us have to go."

I had heard of this tournament before, and I reminded everyone—the competition would be top-notch. We all promised to show up in top physical shape, able to play at least two games a day for five days. Since it was only ten weeks away, we needed to adopt a routine right away to be in top basketball shape.

Everyone thought a moment longer, then quickly reached a unanimous decision. Yes, we were all in! Vacation time? Almost everyone could manage it. Mike at the news station and Craig at Rest In Peace would know within a week.

We would have to hurry to get our application in and reserve a motel. Now that basketball season was over, I agreed to handle these tasks. Craig would secure a sponsor. We agreed that we'd all use our former college numbers. Families? Absolutely! We'd bring our families along. We'd have one big, fun, wild get-together with a huge support base.

We left breakfast, pumped. Dave, Joe, Jim, and I said our goodbyes to the others and headed for the airport. During the flight back, I couldn't help but remember leaving Lakefield College sad and unfulfilled. Could this tournament serve as a catalyst to not only re-bond our group but put to rest all the ghosts from college years past? Was it still possible to put the icing on the proverbial cake—to give it one last try to go out on top and take advantage of this final opportunity to pay Coach back for what he had done for each of us?

But we *were* in our forties. If we did not play up to our hopes ... what then?

THIRTEEN

TEAMS ARE MADE
DURING
THE OFF-SEASON

Over the next few weeks, emails flew through cyberspace. Craig and Mike were in. Our application was accepted. However, we had to prove to the tournament committee members that we could play at this level. I learned that several called Lakefield and checked our backgrounds. Amazingly, I managed to reserve seven motel rooms—all at the hotel we had stayed at eighteen years before. Craig had found us a sponsor who would pay our entry fee and give us uniforms—Craig reported that he had ordered one tiny uniform, five extra large, and one humongous! We routinely emailed each other our workout schedules, along with funny photos—Dave dunking, Rex practicing threes or dozing in a lawn chair poised in the lane, Craig bench-pressing his daughter Abbey. Updating us all constantly with his weight, Rex once mistakenly listed 520 lbs. He quickly re-emailed—It was *250* lbs. The error was due to a transposing of the number—*not* to his latest trip to a buffet!! We counted the days. The families, too, grew excited. All of us would finally meet after having heard about each other for years. Some of the kids made signs for the game. We'd have our very own South Forty!

On July 3 we flew to Orlando. Several of the families were on board. Craig and his family were driving. Rex and Mike would arrive on different flights later in the day. Only two children were missing, Dave's son John and Jim's daughter Becky. It was great to see so many on the flight, but the bigger reunion was yet to come.

We landed, rented three vans, and headed for Deland. It

was amazing to see Stetson again—as beautiful as we had remembered it. Craig and his family had already arrived. We checked into the motel. I drove back to the airport to pick up Rex and Mike. As they exited the restricted area for passenger arrival, I could make out their silhouettes. They were walking with a third person. Someone they had met on the flight? They drew near, and grinned. It was Mike, Rex, and Barb Davis—the Bunny!! I couldn't believe it. Rex laughed—"Uh, brought my date along," he said.

Barb and Rex had been seeing each other for about two months. After graduation Barb had taught at a high school in Green Bay and had been a Packer cheerleader for five years. Rex had bumped into her at a bar in DuPere about four months ago. "I've come down to support the troops," she said—just like in the good old days.

And Rex? Mike looked to me, saw my face, and said, "I was as surprised as you were!"

Yes, it was incredible. Rex was down to 230 lbs.

"I lost twenty-six so far," he explained, obviously happy with his accomplishment. "I hope the, uh, 'tiny' uniform is for me?"

We toted their luggage to the van and loaded it in the back. As I picked up one of Rex's bags, the top came open. Several candy bars and packages of chips and cookies appeared.

I cracked up, but Rex didn't find it funny. He insisted I don't tell anyone. I promised I wouldn't.

On the ride back to Deland we talked of old times,

of our earlier trips to Florida. Barb said she had been to Daytona Beach several times. When she said that, I could only envision the commotion she must have caused on the beach. As we drove on, we approached a railroad sign.

"Hey—R-R. Look at that sign!" called Rex.

"Don't even go there," I said.

We both laughed.

As we pulled in, our troops were all at the pool beside the parking area. They all came running out to greet us. Finally, we all would meet each other. We met for supper at the pool and had pizzas delivered. All the kids had a wonderful time laughing, chasing one another, and enjoying one another's company.

The next day we were up by 7 a.m., with a full schedule and no time to lose. The women and kids were going to Disneyworld for the day, and left early. We ate a quick breakfast and walked over to check the draw. Stetson would use ten outdoor tartan courts for the games, each brand new and with glass backboards. The draw showed only two seeds penciled in. At the top were the High Flyers from Las Vegas. Air Supply from Cleveland was located at the bottom. We were fourth from the top, and would meet Bobby's Ballers from Orlando, in a game slated for 10 a.m. If we won that first game and the High Flyers won theirs, we would meet in the second round. Dave reached up toward the champion line. "When we get up to here," he said, "we'll send a team picture to Coach."

Since it was a double-elimination, the tournament guaranteed each team three games. Rumor held that if you lost your first two, they would put you in a separate bracket—the Toilet Bowl. We must avoid this scenario at all cost!

We practiced for an hour and a half and got in a good, solid workout. We stretched, shot, did some full court drills, and worked on some special plays. Finally, we scrimmaged another early-arriving team from Tennessee. As we played, I couldn't help but notice how fundamentally sound the guys were. Someone, sometime long ago, had taught us well. July in Florida is hot and muggy. We swiftly realized what we were up against more than opposing teams.

Back at the motel we showered, rested for a few hours, and had lunch. We strolled around campus and stopped in the gym where we had defeated Stetson some eighteen years before. There was a youth camp going on. We watched for a time and exchanged small talk with some locals. I learned that Glenn Wilkes, Stetson's coach from 1989, was no longer there. The current coach was Derek Waugh. Wilkes, a Hall of Famer, had coached for thirty-six seasons and had retired after the 1992-93 season. During his tenure, Stetson had won 552 games.

We returned to our rooms, rested for a few hours, and waited for all the others to return. They arrived promptly at 6:00 and requested time to freshen up. We agreed to meet at 6:15 and piled into the vans. We drove to a local burger take-out, ordered, and drove to nearby Lake Helen. Once there, we laid out blankets, ate, and watched the fireworks over the lake. The kids thought they were in heaven. My daughter Kim named a special firework for each of us. After the show we drove back and prepared for a good night's sleep. Tomorrow would be a big day, full of challenges.

With the 7 a.m. wake-up call, butterflies invaded my stomach—just like in college. It was a jolt, a feeling that I loved and missed. I kissed Terry and the kids goodbye and hurried to meet the others for breakfast. By 7:30 a.m. we were together.

"Hey Rex—did you get any sleep?" Dave asked.

Everyone chuckled, but I could tell that jokes would be limited. We had agreed to take this outing seriously and put forth our best effort.

After we discussed a few general items and finished eating, Craig pulled out a box that contained the uniforms and began to hand them out. As we opened the cellophaned packages, we spied our old numbers, then our sponsor's name just above. We were in shock. The name we'd be known as all week was—REST IN PEACE. We braced ourselves for the inevitable, knowing our jerseys would spark crowd reaction. Dave imitated a corpse. Joe made the sign of the cross. Rex said it reminded him of Northeastern Illinois—time for a smell test.

We told Craig that we appreciated the sponsorship, but said so tongue-in-cheek. We quickly changed, and with our sweatshirts over our jerseys headed to the court to view the last half of the 8 a.m. games. Around 9:30 a.m. we began to stretch, warm up, and shoot around. At 9:55 a.m. we were called to the scorer's table for the five-minute warm-up.

10 a.m. It was time for Lakefield's best, Andrews's RIP, to take the floor against Bobby's Ballers from Orlando. We were determined to put our past behind us, to finish our careers on a high note and erase our mediocre ending. We shed our warm-up tops and displayed our uniforms. Rebirth? Such would seem against the odds with "REST IN PEACE" on our chests.

We lined up for the center jump, to a yell from who appeared to be a fan of the opposing team—"Let's put these guys in the grave."

Their fans laughed. We looked at each other, and laughed. We would be hearing this for the next five days, we knew. The ref tossed up the ball. The Undertaker leaped high and tipped me the ball. I immediately passed it off to Dave.

With the Ballers in a man-to-man defense, the Midget set us up accordingly. We ran "Under," a play designed to get the ball immediately inside. Craig received the ball at the high post, squared up, and made a short lob to Rex, who had sealed his man beautifully. Rex scored easily: RIP 2, Ballers 0.

The South "Twenty" cheered. Terry screamed. The Bunny shook and rocked. We quickly saw that we had a definite height advantage. We would take advantage of it.

We worked to a 20-12 lead, due mostly to the inside game. With three minutes left in the fifteen minute half, we stretched our lead to 36-19. To provide inside help, the Ballers had started to sag on defense. As they covered down, our inside people would fan the ball back out for easy jumpers. The shots were falling. We seemed to be hitting on all cylinders. Everyone was contributing and scoring with ease.

The thirty-second shot clock kept the game moving, to our advantage. We led at the half, 42-22. In the second half we elected to go to a zone to conserve energy and make them shoot strictly from the outside. To win this tournament, it was far less important how much you won by than making sure you conserved your energy for your next game. Considering the weather and the number of games to finish, we would have to pace ourselves. We didn't play as well the second half, but solid enough to win, 73-48.

Our cheering section was elated, and we were relieved. We had a fine first showing. Rex led the team with twenty points. Craig had fourteen, and Joe and I each had twelve. We got something to drink and came back to scout the High Flyers, who would play on the same court at 11:00, against Boston's Birds.

After watching the first half, we were duly impressed. The High Flyers were up 39-21. We could see how they had claimed the championship for the last two years. Nonetheless, we felt we had a great chance. We matched up with them very well. They played a game quite similar to ours.

We headed out to dry our uniforms and get some lunch and a little rest. We would play at 4 p.m., very likely against the High Flyers. We were elated to have had a good start.

Mathematically, there was no way we would advance to the Toilet Bowl. We would return to the court at 3:30 p.m. to stretch and shoot. As our team's player/coach, I, like the others, felt confident about the match-ups and our game plan.

Our entire contingent made its way to the courts at 3:30 p.m., all excited to see how well we would do against last year's champs. There was a large crowd. The High Flyers always drew audiences due to their success.

As we positioned ourselves for the opening tip, we again heard a heckler—"Go, Flyers! Bury these guys!!" The voice seemed to be the heckler's from the earlier game. We laughed. Even the High Flyers grinned.

The game started methodically, each team feeling the other out. A very quick team, the Flyers got some fine looks off individual moves, but their shots weren't falling. At the same time, we couldn't get the ball inside, as they were covering down with their guards and playing their big men behind our post players. This gave us some great looks from the outside, and we hit four of our first five shots. We now led, 10-4. The difference in the early game was simple—the ability to hit the open shot.

At this point the High Flyers worked hard to get the ball inside. Using a high–low with their posts off an initial cross-screen, they were able to get some better looks and scored on four straight possessions. As we sagged off their outside people to help in the paint, they fanned the ball back out and started to hit their outside shots. With four and a half minutes left, the score was tied, 29-29. For the rest of the half, each team boosted defensive pressure to take a halftime lead. Right after a timeout, the Flyers ran a backdoor Alley Oop for a dunk, and ran off the floor very pumped: Flyers 37, RIP 35. We had only a short five-minute break to dissect the game and adjust. We had played a fine all-around half, and the match-ups seemed appropriate. Maybe we should throw in some zone or cover down on their 6'9" center, Evans. He was a real beast on the boards and already had 12 points at the half. We decided to begin the second half with our man-to-man half-court defense.

The second half was a very clean game, with few turnovers. We got good looks initially, but as time went on they forced us to shoot more from the perimeter. We would penetrate and, as they provided help, kick the ball out. They would rush to the ball, and we would swing it to the open man. At the beginning we hit our shots, but with six minutes left the score was 62-56, Flyers. We tried to run some special plays for easier attempts, but their defense made it difficult. The Flyers then shifted into a one–four offense. They kept the ball in the hands of their quick point guard, Williams, stationed at the top of the key, and positioned four players across on the baseline. He would penetrate and take the Midget off the bounce, in an effort to attack the rim. If we provided help, he would pitch the ball to a post player or fan it to a wing for a shot. His passes were precise, as if he were performing surgery on our defense. This offensive scheme made it difficult for us to provide help, and their lead grew to ten points with two minutes to go. We full-court-pressed, forced a turnover, but ended up putting them on the line several times. Composed, they made their shots. With a minute and a half left and up by twelve, they went into a stall. We were almost out of gas, and could only continue to foul. Hitting their last six free throws, they coasted to a 74-60 victory.

The crowd cheered both teams. It had been a intense, high-level game involving some fine strategy. Mike and I each had 16 points to lead our effort.

Day One was over. We were 1-1, and feeling dejected. I don't ever think we ever anticipated losing a game.

We found a shady spot under a large palm tree and sat down. It was double-elimination, but now our backs were to the wall. We agreed. This loss was too reminiscent of our last game in college. It was *uncanny* how closely it mirrored that sad memory. We didn't meet the challenge defensively. We didn't execute offensively when we needed to. We hadn't been able to manufacture many transition points. Even the High flyer players were remarkably identical in stature to Central Wisconsin's. Like Central Wisconsin, the High Flyers were a very talented bunch. They had players from UNLV, UCLA, Pepperdine, San Diego State, and Nevada-Reno. Nonetheless, at times during the game our team play far exceeded their individual talents. We just didn't sustain it for the whole thirty minutes. We had been out-rebounded, had allowed penetration, had settled for too many threes, and had failed to run our offensive sets. We had come down to end our past—and now had only a sad reminder.

What was the missing element? How could we become that team we had always wanted to be? We needed an answer, very soon. The Flyers were on top. We had to find a way out of the losers' bracket to play them again. Our next game would be at 11 a.m. tomorrow against the Indianapolis Rebounders.

That night all the tournament families attended a barbeque. The kids played with Frisbees and hula hoops provided by Deland Recreation. Hamburgers, hot dogs, and Sheboygan bratwurst with all the fixings were plentiful. We sat around, ate, and for long hours talked—a fine opportunity to bond. I could tell each wife or girlfriend knew how much this endeavor meant to us. How supportive they were! The night together relaxed us all. We retired early for a great night's sleep—a perfect recipe.

We slept in and met for breakfast about 9 a.m. We were looser and somewhat over our defeat by the Flyers. We knew it was now or never. Somewhat philosophical, we headed over to the courts to warm up.

Our tip-off against the Rebounders was at 11 a.m. This was the first game that didn't debut with the Heckler. Was he merely taking the day off, or resting his sore throat?

The game started slowly. We played a quarter-court man-to-man; they, a zone defense that at times resembled a 2-1-2 and at other times a 2-3. Either way, we began with our gap-hold offense and changed to "Gap Movement" in about six minutes. "Gap Hold" was a 1-3-1 offensive formation, where our perimeter players would stay in the same general area. When the short corner and post would move side to side it produced some great looks. We could pass to the short corner, who would dump it to a post man diving for the basket. If they covered down with their guards, our short corner could fan the ball back out and we could penetrate the gap and swing the ball for fine opportunities. When they got used to this movement, we resorted to our gap-movement offense. Our wings would pass and go opposite, our big men would cross. As the ball moved side to side, the short corner would become the high post, the high post would become the short corner. Easy to run, this offense was difficult to defend. We quickly built a 14-point lead.

The Rebounders continued to zone until halftime, with the score 38-22, RIP. We zoned a bit ourselves in the second half in an effort to force them into outside shots and reserve ourselves physically. Both teams playing zones kept the score down, and the game went by quickly. Even with our late twenty-point lead, the Rebounders continued their zone, and we won, 66-48. Rex had 14 points, Craig and Joe each scored 12. I had 10.

We were pleased with our effort. We would play at 6 p.m., the day's late game, against the Chicago Bull's Eyes whom everyone touted as speed-demons. Having seen them play, we knew they loved to full-court-press. We rested, had our uniforms washed, and planned dinner at 4 p.m. There we talked about our press-breaker and our options. They wanted to play a very fast, full-court game. This we knew. We had to slow them down.

FOURTEEN

THE DIFFERENCE BETWEEN ORDINARY AND EXTRAORDINARY IS JUST THAT LITTLE 'EXTRA'

T his game, too, tipped off right on time. We were all a bit stiff, but we knew almost all the other players were feeling much the same. Our game plan was perfect. Immediately they used a full-court zone press to get us in a run-and-gun game. To answer this tactic, we would inbound the ball, reverse it, and then get it to the middle. We kept our cool and easily broke their press.

When they brought more pressure on the inbounds pass, we brought up Rex and Craig in a spread formation and threw them the inbounds passes. One thing we had stressed in our prep for breaking the press was taking only high-percentage shots. Just because we broke free did not warrant a wild shot. For the most part we adhered to this philosophy and the game played into our hands. If we didn't get a great look, we pulled the ball out and made them play defense, and we built a halftime lead of 38-27.

The second half started much the same, but they were now pressing full-court and man-to-man. We continued to get the ball in to Rex and Craig, who would then pass it back to Dave or me to work our way up the court. Even though setting up our half-court offense left us only about twenty seconds on the shot clock, it was plenty of time to run our motion offense and, after four or five passes, get a clean shot. Playing consistently, we won, 70-58. Joe had 16 points; Jim, 14 ; Dave, 10.

Day Two was now in the books. We were 2-0 for the day, 3-1 over all. We felt better—much better—about our play, especially that we had used our heads to beat a quicker opponent.

We scanned the draw. The High Flyers had won easily— 80-61 and 79-48. We seemed to have given them their toughest contest. Rex mentioned that, if we came up from the back draw, we would have to beat the Flyers twice, since it was a double-elimination tournament.

We showered, sat around the pool, dipped our feet in the Jacuzzi. After some snacks, we retired early, faced with playing the early game the following day at 8 a.m.

Six o'clock came quickly. Our rooting section decided to take a needed break and spend the day at Daytona Beach. Terry expected to come home and find us 2-0. I assured her that we would not let them down. We said goodbye, and I went to join the others at the coffee shop to eat. We were quite pumped with our efforts of the day before. We had improved mentally and were playing with the necessary sense of urgency. However, we still needed to take our game to another level. If we continued to improve with each game, we *would* be right where we wanted to be at the end. Above all, we had to focus on team play and decision-making. This morning, we'd meet the Denver Dunkers, 3-1, just like us. We had played no common opponent. Up to this point we had alternated our starters, but moving forward we'd keep the same lineup. Rex, Craig, Dave, Jim, and I would be the starters. Mike and Joe would come off the bench, just as they had at Lakefield. We found it ironic that we made the same decision as Luby did eighteen years before—and probably for the same reasons. Mike and Joe were very good off the bench, and their ability to play several positions was a huge bonus.

As the game started, our heckler made a return visit, this time yelling, "Get the dead meat off the floor!" and "It's time for a Denver sandwich!" We tried not to react, but I caught a few smirks from my teammates.

Denver came out in a 1-3-1 half-court trap. As the ball penetrated the top of the key, they reduced to a quarter-court 1-3-1, no longer trapping. It was a smart defense, since their team had good height and ample wingspans but lacked speed. We set up in a box set, with Craig in the middle. We first had to break through their trap, just over half court. We would bring our two guards up quickly to half court without crossing, then fake a pass and return the ball crosscourt to the other guard. This would allow an easy entry pass to Rex in the middle or either Craig or Jim in the corners. Once the first pass was made, we would swiftly pass the ball to our teammates and penetrate.

Ball fakes and skip passes were executed with precision. We could almost hear Luby's voice echo, "Even if there is no one to pass to behind a defensive player, he does not know it and will retreat on a fake." We successfully moved the ball side to side, and, once Craig established post-position on the ball side low block, we flashed the opposite baseline player to the high post to create looks. Even though our alignment worked, the time it took to break down the defense was problematic. Most often we would get jump shots as opposed to working the ball inside. Great patience was imperative. While we managed to hit a decent percentage, when we did miss they had great rebound positions and limited any second-chance opportunities. On their end of the court we resorted to a man-to-man defense and were now covering down on their posts.

It became a chess game. Instinctively we knew the team who could hit the most outside jumpers would have the upper hand. The halftime score was tied, 29-29. At the break we emphasized patience. Most of the teams were not alternating defenses, so we anticipated more of the same, 1-3-1. Defensively, we decided to play honest on their wings, front the posts, and provide "help defense" on the lob. We would challenge them to score inside.

The game continued to be close. We led, 56-55, with two minutes remaining. On two consecutive possessions their 6'9" center hit a short jump hook and an eight-foot jumper off the glass, giving them a three-point lead. We brought the ball down, worked it to Rex in the middle. He fanned it to Mike, who sank a three from the corner. With forty-five seconds left, the score was once again tied, 59-59.

The Dunkers, a patient team, worked the clock down to thirteen seconds before taking a corner shot. The ball bounced off the rim and out toward the middle. Craig secured the rebound and quickly called timeout. As play continued, we looked for the trap and got the ball to Craig in the corner. With six seconds left, he skipped the ball cross-court diagonally to me on the opposite wing. I caught the ball, faked a shot, and fanned the ball to Joe in the corner, his sweet spot. With two seconds left, he squared up and let go an eighteen-footer—good!

We survived! We all hugged Joe, who, with a wide smirk, broke into his impression. "Rainman bring J to Florida. Rainman like road trip. Yah, who's on first?" he mumbled. We cracked up. It was time to put our feet up and get some rest. It was already 91 degrees and very humid. Our next game would be at 2 p.m., the opponent yet undetermined. We were anxious to scout the 10 a.m. game. We would meet the winner of the clash between the Seattle Slammers and Milwaukee Maulers. At this point only two teams had no losses—the Portland Powerhouse and the High Flyers.

We all rested under a shady orange tree as Joe went to his room and retrieved drinks. We propped our legs up and let our jerseys dry in the sun. Just after 10 a.m. we convened at Court Seven. The game was very competitive, but it quickly grew apparent that the Seattle Slammers' talent—three former major college players conspicuous by their abilities—lent them the upper hand. They, too, played very well together as a team. With seven minutes left and the Slammers ahead, 58-44, their point guard brought the ball up to set up their offense. As he dribbled toward the right wing, their Two Man (shooting guard) tried to banana-cut towards the free-throw line. Seeing his path blocked, he turned back the other way toward his point guard, as if to run a weave. As he rounded the corner he ran smack into the point guard who was not expecting his reverse cut.

The collision left both players on the floor, dazed from the impact. Both sustained cuts to their foreheads, mirror images of each other. The game was delayed as both players, bleeding heavily, made their way to the sideline and then to the local hospital. The Seattle team had only five players left to finish the game; two of their three stars were gone. Sensing the change, Milwaukee immediately pressed, caused several turnovers, and seemed to control the game. To stop the momentum, the Slammers used their timeouts. Their 14-point lead was now 6, with a minute and a half to go. The Slammers went into a stall, firing up a shot only to beat the shot clock, with 58 seconds left. The shot grazed the rim, but bounced directly back to the shooter, who pulled back out for a fresh shot clock, and held on for a 68-64 victory.

The Slammers were pleased with their victory, but their mood was somber. The status of their injured teammates for the 2 p.m. game was definitely questionable.

We left for lunch with our minds racing. The Slammers would be a far better team with everyone present. Rex asked, "If they are down to only five players, should we press like Milwaukee? Would it be fair?" We felt bad for the Slammers and discussed the issue at some length. Most of us agreed that, if we lost two players to foul trouble or just not showing up, any team would take advantage. Sports are competitive and teams take advantage of opportunities. We decided to start out in a half-court man-to-man defense and shift to a full-court press shortly after. However, everything would depend on their lineup. At 1:50 p.m. we took the court to warm up. At the other end only five players were practicing, and none of their fans was present.

The game started. We got the tip, worked for a solid shot inside, and Rex hit a short jump hook. We retreated and picked them up at half court, as planned. Everyone played tough defense, with great pressure on the ball, and we stopped them on their first six possessions. Additionally, we scored on four of our next six and led by a score of 11-0. We were playing great, with a lot of confidence.

They took a quick time out to stop our run. We decided not to press. I think we all came out playing hard so we would not have to consider pressing their depleted team. The game continued. Our lead grew. By halftime we were up 32-15. As we came off the court, our families were there to greet us. They had left the beach earlier than planned. They had heard about our first victory and wanted to support us.

In the second half the Slammers ran a zone, but it was porous and we were efficient. With nine minutes left, they shifted back to a man-to-man, but we could see they were exhausted. We won, 63-42.

Being able to rest during part of the game with our seven players had been a factor, but also we had played extremely well. We congratulated the Slammers and commended their effort. We told them we were sorry about the circumstances.

The loss of the two players had been their downfall. Each had received several stitches and was recuperating in his room. The team thanked us and wished us luck.

We were elated. We hadn't had to use our press and play the bad guy. We had won with honor. As the names and scores were added to the draw, we noticed that the High Flyers had won easily, 80-54. They would play game two at 5. It appeared that we still had been their toughest opponent. Now, three days into the tournament, we were 5-1. Two days remained. We hoped to play three more games. If we were to make it to the final matched against an undefeated team, we would have to beat them twice for the championship. Tomorrow would be our last two-game day. We would need to be ready and play solid basketball. Our opponent for the 9 a.m. game? The Portland Powerhouse.

We were now ready to celebrate, at least for the short term. We quickly cleaned up. Then the whole group went out for Mexican food. It had been a great day. The families had enjoyed a diversion, while we had taken care of business on the court. Everyone was in a festive mood. It was nothing short of amazing to see our families evolving into a team. The kids all got along. The older ones acted as little parents for the younger. The wives seemed to have a great rapport. Surprisingly, the Bunny fit in well, and proved to be a favorite with the kids. Everyone could see that she was extremely intelligent. Her physical attributes paled when compared to her caring, loving disposition.

FIFTEEN

TRIUMPH IS JUST 'UMPH' ADDED TO TRY

Day Four: Physically, we had fared well. We were one of only a few teams with everyone completely healthy. Our individual preparation before the tournament—that was the key. We had promised one another that we would arrive in shape, and we had.

We ate breakfast at 7 a.m. and arrived courtside by 8:30 a.m. The scorer's table was mobbed by buzzing, murmuring fans. Soon we, too, were shocked: The High Flyers had been beaten in last night's late game, 49-47. The officials told us that two of their stars had flown back to Las Vegas for business and had missed the action, but would be back for their next game. The team had played with six.

Now we were pumped, and our adrenalin really kicked into high gear. All the teams in the final eight had one loss. If we could survive this morning, we'd make the final four. The four games would begin at 9 a.m.

Our opponent, the Portland Powerhouse, was already warming up. Our attention turned to the center, the tournament's only 7' player. Craig insisted that he was still a "project" and wouldn't present a problem. Portland's large fan base had accompanied the team all the way from the Pacific Northwest. Their fans were already present and noisy. On the other side of the court, our families made their way up into the bleachers. We took the floor at 8:40 a.m., for a great, invigorating warm-up. A great opportunity lay before us. We felt prepared.

The game began precisely at 9 a.m. The center jump matched Craig against the 7-footer. Craig looked tiny in comparison. Even though Craig was 2 inches shorter than Rex, we had chosen him because he could get up much quicker and higher. "Here we go, gentlemen"—the ref tossed up the ball. Their center easily tipped it to his teammate, who handed it off to the point guard to set the offense.

We retreated into a man-to-man. Rex fronted the big post player. As they moved the ball side to side to take away our weak-side help and lob the ball in, we hustled, forced an outside shot, and crashed the boards. Craig secured the rebound and passed it off. Dave moved quickly, and took the ball down the court against their transition defense. Everyone got back quickly, even the big guy. We tried our secondary break, but they covered that as well. They were talking on defense. It was obvious we had been scouted, big time. Dave adjusted and called a special, "Double." Jim hit a three, and we hustled back on defense.

Both teams played extremely aggressively and as a result, committed several fouls. The Power House seemed to be trying to intimidate us. Both of the cheering sections howled on each call, adding to the mounting tension. It was a low-scoring game, as each team had to work the ball to get a decent shot. The fouls increased. Determined to not let the game get out of hand, the refs continued to use their whistles. With two minutes left in the half and with three fouls each, Craig and Rex were forced to the bench.

That put Joe at the center position. My long three-pointer bounced high off the rim. Joe blocked out the big guy perfectly. He reached over in spite and, as one would say, got his hand caught in the cookie jar, committing his third foul. He, too, left the game. We now had a fresh 30-second clock for the last shot of the half. This time we ran "Double" to the other side. With eight seconds left, Dave penetrated and kicked it back to Jim, who nailed a three.

The half ended with us leading, 33-27. Craig, Rex and Joe had three fouls each. Portland's big man also had three, as did their point guard. Our lead was the result of hitting six of nine three-pointers. We couldn't count on such a percentage continuing.

In an effort to minimize fouls, both teams reverted to zone defenses (2-1-2's) in the second half. We began with our gap-hold offense, a 1-3-1 alignment with Craig moving from side to side or short corner to short corner, and quickly ran a play called "Over." As Dave at the top of the key received a return pass from the wing, he took two hard dribbles toward the other wing. As he did, instead of racing to the other ball side short corner, Craig sealed the low man on the weak side of the zone. Jim then dropped to the corner in time to receive a skip pass back over the entire zone defense from Dave. The play produced a great open look—and another three-pointer. The next time down on offense, we got the ball to Craig in the short corner. Rex dove to the hoop and received a flip pass from Craig, then two-hand-dunked the ball with emphasis, with the opposing center hanging on his back. Their big guy now had four fouls. Rex's free throw put us up by twelve. We had hoped that our early success against the zone would entice them to go back to man-to-man, but, with the big man's fourth foul and despite our twelve-point lead, they were not going to change.

The next twelve minutes were played evenly. We continued to work the ball against their zone, they against ours. We kept the double-digit lead and limited fouling to a bare minimum. The refs' calling early fouls had certainly changed the game. With seven minutes to go and the clock now a critical element, Portland finally shifted into a man-to-man defense. They could no longer allow thirty seconds to expire with each possession and needed to force the action. We went into our motion offense and, defensively, stayed in our zone.

We took a quick timeout to review: We were up by eleven, and had possession of the ball. We decided to stay in the zone, force the outside shot, and give them only single attempts. Offensively, we would make at least five passes, utilize the shot clock, work for good shot. Timeouts? We had one remaining.

The action proceeded as planned. At the two-minute mark we still had a ten-point lead, and ran "Melt" for the duration. They fouled us to stop the clock. We hit five of six from the charity stripe. By the end we had lost only Craig to fouls and won, 65-54. I had scored 16; Joe and Mike, 14; Craig, 10.

Our team and fans were ecstatic. What had started out as a pool of eighty-eight teams was now down to four. We congratulated Portland, and made our way to recheck the draw, which had been updated. The St. Louis Shooters had just beaten Seattle's finest, 71-62. The Dayton Demolition Team had defeated the Houston Hoops, 62-56. The High Flyers had eliminated the Providence Players, 68-54. The semis, set for 2 p.m. today, would match Dayton and the Flyers—RIP and the St. Louis Shooters.

We wished we could have scouted the St. Louis-Seattle game. It had not been possible—we had been playing at the same time. Overhearing our discussion, Barb came over with a video for Rex. "Here you go, honey," she said. "I got the first two thirds of the St Louis game. I couldn't take it any more, and had to come and catch the end of your game."

Rex grinned. "Hey, guys—time to catch some TV?"

We showered quickly and gathered in Rex's room. Joe's wife Monica volunteered to wash the uniforms, claiming that she would scrub the name off, if possible. It took Rex twenty minutes of adjusting to get the game to show. "Where is Ev when we need him?" kidded Dave.

We studied the tape intently, as if preparing for a final exam. Hey—we were! St. Louis was a solid team. We'd have to bring our A-game. They liked to change defenses often, so we had to pay extra attention. Their loss had been to Houston, by only one point. They had eight players—four from D-I teams—and they all seemed in top physical shape. We were determined. We would put all we had into this game. A loss would mean no tomorrow.

As we finished watching, we heard someone yell in the background. Barb zoomed in. We got a good look. The voice was familiar. He looked like Don Rickles.

"Hey, that's the guy who's been yelling at *our* games."

Barb walked in. "You even got the famous heckler," Rex said.

Barb laughed. "I knew you guys would like that."

She went on to say that she had talked to the guy, who is a comedian—a Don Rickles impersonator. "Told you guys," grinned Joe. Barb explained that the guy worked at a club in Orlando and was a basketball fanatic. He had come up with several ideas for his act from this "Geritol Tournament" as he termed it. Barb had told him that we had heard him at several of our games. He tried to be fair, he said. He spread his criticism evenly among *all* the teams. Barb told us she might hire him for our game.

We would meet at the coffee shop for lunch at 12:30 p.m., when I would finalize our game plan and list all my recommendations. Until then we would stay off our feet.

The hours slipped away, and we leisurely made our way to the court. Surprisingly, many eliminated teams were still there. Most had planned to stay until tomorrow in hopes of making the finals. The players were cordial and wished us luck. The last four days had turned us into a fraternity. I liked that. We all sought the title, yes, but at day's end we respected each other and, out of a deep common interest, had forged a common bond.

At 1:40 p.m. we took the court. We quickly worked up a sweat. A large crowd had gathered at Courts 2 and 4. "Two minutes!" called the refs. We retired to the sideline. We were pumped and ready to go. After a few last-minute remarks, we put our hands together and yelled, "Solid start!"

At once a familiar voice broke out—"Hey St. Louis—watch your arch!!"

Had the Bunny obtained his services?

We lined up. The game started. Craig tapped the ball right to Dave, who pivoted and yelled "Motion!" We set up our man-to-man offense. It only took four passes to get the ball to Mike—a fine opportunity in the post. He pump-faked, stepped through, banked in a six-footer: 2-0.

We sprinted back, filled the lanes, dug in on defense. The Shooters ran a play called Louisville. They hit their high-post player guarded by Craig with the initial pass and sent two cutters off the ball. As the second player hustled by, Craig tipped the ball from his man, picked it up and passed it directly to Dave, who hit a sprinting Mike in perfect stride for a fast break lay-up: 4-0.

For the rest of the half we played terrifically on both ends, making some great plays and dominating the boards. Our screens were outstanding, giving us the separation for open shots. Hitting a blistering 64%, we led at the half, 38-22.

The guys were excited and pleased. Without the great shooting, though, it would be a far closer game. I pointed out that we needed to continue to play solid defense and limit them to one shot. St. Louis was determined but, with all our open looks, they would have to improve defensively.

They began the half with an intensely pressured, full-court man-to-man defense. A few costly turnovers gave them the confidence they sought. By the 10-minute mark they were down by only seven, 50-43. We called a time-out to regroup. They were forcing us to play too quickly. Thinking too much about our shots had caused our percentages to drop significantly.

At the four-minute mark we called our last timeout, up by only two, 61-59. They had made a major surge and were playing far too confidently. We threw in some zone to shake things up, but it did not faze them. They answered with two long threes. Now we needed *our* confidence back and to play with more poise. We were distraught. Their fans were going crazy. Ours were subdued.

We decided to be the aggressor with our man-to-man defense, a tactic yielding mixed results. The next three minutes produced five lead changes. With 1:20 left, the score was tied, 73-73. We had the ball.

We ran "Melt." With 54 seconds left Rex posted and took a turn-around J—which caromed off to St. Louis, who quickly brought the ball down for a spread offense. Considering the shot clock, they would have to fire the ball up by the 22-second mark. At 29 seconds, they positioned four people along the baseline and isolated their point guard at the top of the key. He would take Dave one on one. He put the ball on the floor, started to stutter-dribble, faked left, went right. Dave anticipated the move beautifully and slid in front of him. As their guard gathered himself for a shot, the collision drew a whistle. The ref signaled a foul on Dave and awarded their player two free throws.

Both crowds shrieked and cheered loudly, with only 24 seconds left on the clock. As their player went to the line, Dave yelled, "Motion to Lancer!," designating our next set when we got possession. Their guard bounced the ball hard three times, carefully lined up his shot, and released. The ball spun on the rim for a few seconds, then fell off. He stepped away momentarily, edged back onto the line, readied himself a second time, and took three more dribbles. The shot bounced off the rim's left side, into Rex's waiting hands. Dave ran to Rex, ripped the ball away, yelled, "Go!" Everyone sprinted off. We had our alignment set, reached our spots. With 12 seconds remaining Dave repeated, "Go!" and dribbled to the foul line extended on the left. His defender reached in, caught his arm, drew a whistle.

With the Shooters over the limit, Dave, a 90% free-throw shooter, had earned two chances from the line. What had earlier been a moment of sheer despair now turned into a moment of hope. Ten seconds remained.

Dave lined up, took a deep breath, readied himself, took two dribbles, and let fly. The ball hit the rim softly, and rolled off. Their fans cheered. Ours groaned. Dave, visibly disgusted, retreated from the line. We all shouted encourage-ment. It was okay. Dave prepared the second shot. The ball left his hand right on line—and went through the basket by only slightly moving the net. Our fans jumped to their feet, cheering loudly.

Out of timeouts, with time only for a quick shot, St.

Louis brought the ball down and settled for long three. The ball bounced off the rim. Craig jumped high, knocked the rebound far into the crowd—to the sound of the horn.

We had survived. We had done it! We had made it to the finals. As a sea of our fans rushed onto the floor in support, we congratulated the Shooters on their effort. They wished us the best of luck. Yes, we had survived, but with a major blow to our confidence. Did we belong in the final? Really belong? We had been very lucky to win the game. This we knew. The other semi-final had been decisive—a High Flyers victory, 75-56, over Dayton. Tomorrow's noon championship game would match the twice-defending-champ High Flyers from Las Vegas against Anderson's Rest in Peace from Wisconsin.

SIXTEEN

HE WHO FORGIVES
ENDS THE QUARREL

B ack on day one we had decided that if we reached the finals, we would all celebrate with dinner at Ryan's Family Steak House. This would be our last night together. We would each be leaving tomorrow on our separate journeys. We wanted to make it special. We planned to use the party room so our group could have some privacy. Terry announced that the reservation was set—she had made it four days ago. We all laughed.

First, the team needed to meet to review today's play and plan for tomorrow's game. We cleaned up and met by the pool. It was apparent. Everyone was upset by our less-than-stellar performance an hour before. I decided to venture the lead.

"The good news is that we got it out of our system," I said, "But honestly guys, there is something missing in our play. We *didn't finish*. It had nothing to do with us physically—it was mental!!"

All agreed. We opened the forum for suggestion. Yes, we must focus on each moment and execute each play as if it were our last. We needed to be more supportive of each other and do "the little things" so needed, especially when not directly involved in the play at hand.

Finally Joe asked, "I wonder what Luby would think?"

There was a moment of silence.

Then, Mike ventured—"You guys thinking what I'm thinking?"

Jim looked around. "Let's give him a call, invite him down. If he can't make it, at least he'll know we were thinking about him. Kentucky? That's not that far from here— right?"

Since his retirement, Coach and Shirley were living in Paducah, Kentucky, right on the lake. Paducah was a dream site Coach had often referred to through the years. It was a town in McCracken County, in the western part of the state, with absolutely first-rate fishing. During one difficult game my freshman year, Coach had quipped that if we continued to play at this level there would be good news and bad news. The bad news: An early retirement would be looming. The good news: The retiree would be hooking a large bass in Paducah, Kentucky.

Jim would call, and tell us about it at dinner.

Tomorrow's game would be a classic match-up; a group of greatly talented individuals who were two time defending national champs and a group whose best asset was (hopefully) the way they approached the game of basketball as a team. We set our game plan and decided to open up in a man-to-man defense. I showed the guys "Chameleon," a strategy I had devised. It would confuse a team's offensive alignment and ability to get good shots. As the team set up its offense, we would quickly adjust our defensive alignment on its first pass. This, we felt, had merit, especially against the High Flyers. Previously, we had run only three special plays on offense. Tomorrow would warrant several more. We all agreed that the whole team would benefit with a good night's sleep. It was now 4:30 p.m.—time to leave for Ryan's.

We were escorted into a cozy, private room with one long table. Floor-to-ceiling glass showcased a breathtaking view of freshly manicured green grass, hibiscus, azaleas, and majestic queen palms. On one end of the table stood a podium. Our families had decorated the room earlier in the day with blue and gold balloons and streamers—Lakefield's colors. What a festive occasion!

Through the side door, we could view the bar—and Mike animatedly chatting with a female bartender. Dave and I went to fetch him. He rose with, "Julie—see you later." Dave and I rolled our eyes.

Once seated, we decided that everyone would say a few words before we ate. Jim was eager to go first to give us an update:

"I called Coach's house. Shirley answered and told me Coach was sleeping. I told her about the tournament and asked if she and Coach could come to the final game tomorrow. She sounded sad, and told me that Coach wasn't doing very well. He had a very difficult time walking. She did not think that they would be able to join us. She told me that she would be sure to tell Coach that I called, and wished everyone her best. She added that she would even say a special prayer for our success tomorrow." He paused for a moment. "So I was thinking: *If*—I mean *when*—we win tomorrow, we should send the trophy to Luby. What do you think?"

Everyone quickly agreed.

Next, Mike spoke. "As the only one down here without family, I want to thank all of you. I have enjoyed your friendship and feel like I am part of one 'large family.' Someday I'd love to have what you all have—a family of my own."

He continued. "I have some exciting news to share with you. I have an interview scheduled tomorrow morning at 8 a.m. for the weekend-anchor spot at WFTV, Channel 9. Orlando is a much larger market, so this would be a huge promotion for me. I'll be back in plenty of time for the game. I PROMISE."

"Don't pull a High Flyer!!" Dave shouted.

"I won't. This game means a lot to all of us. I won't let you down."

It was now my turn to say a few words. "The last few days have brought back great memories of playing college ball together. This week we created some new memories. We renewed old friendships and made new ones with all our extended families. I hope that we will stay in close contact. Tomorrow will be a big day for *all* of us. After it's over, we can all FINALLY rest in peace."

Dave went next. He surveyed the room, and then asked, "Why am I the only one that looks the same after all these years?"

We all laughed. "Probably because you never grew!" retorted Rex.

Everyone laughed, howled.

"Rex, tell your dad—uh, the heckler—to take it easy on us tomorrow!" answered Dave, to more laughter.

Dave held up his hands. The room fell still. With a

straight face so uncharacteristic of comic Dave, he told the group, "This has been a very special time for me. I knew it would be fun, but the past few days have really exceeded anything I had anticipated. I am proud to be in the company of so many classy players and people. And most importantly, I am SO glad that I hit that clutch free throw!"

Joe broke in with his impression. Assuming the crazy look, he said, "Rainman like tournament. Rainman like dinner. Yah, who's on first?"

Again everyone broke into laughter, especially the kids, who up to this point had only heard of his antics.

"Rainman appreciate everyone. *Everyone*. You are all 'first' in my book!"

He smiled and sat down.

Rex stood up. "First of all, I would like to thank the one responsible for choosing this eating establishment. 'Steak' is one of my *favorite* words. So far it's been a great week—and it's going to get better tomorrow. Cuz—we're going to bring home the gold!" To shrieks and cheers, he shook his fist in the air, then called for silence.

"I have one more announcement I think is appropriate for here and now. About ten minutes ago Barb—accepted my proposal of marriage."

Again, cheers broke out. He stepped over, gave Barb a generous kiss. Wow, we all thought. What a *night*!

Next came Joe, officially. "Top that? I can't. *No one* could." He continued. "Like Rex, I feel victory is close at hand. Our 'team' will make a difference. I want to thank each of you for your support not only now but through the years. Even though we didn't physically talk, I knew each of you was always there. That meant a lot to me. Tomorrow—will be our day!"

Finally, Craig stood up. "I don't think any of you know it yet, but within the next month I will become—an ordained minister. I have thought about this path for a number of years. I am finally making the move." He reached into his pocket, pulled out a paper, and unfolded it. "I'd like to say grace," he offered.

We bowed our heads. He read:

"Dear God, we thank you for our many blessings. We ask that You bless our families, our friends, the food we are about to eat. We thank You for this very special time together and for the gifts You constantly provide. Help us remember the needy. May Your unconditional love consume us, so that we may all share in Your glory."

After a moment, he added, "I'd also like to say a prayer for tomorrow," prompting Dave to yell "Make it a good one, Strap"—in reference to the emotional locker-room scene from *Hoosiers*.

Hoots and yells erupted. Craig smiled, then turned serious once again. As he spoke, the room grew so quiet that we could have heard the proverbial pin drop. No longer with a script, he spoke from his heart:

"Dear God, we thank You for the gift of the reunion of our friendship. We acknowledge how far we have come as individuals. With Your help, we have transformed our individual talents into a strong, powerful, wonderful team. Help us to continue to believe in one another as we believe in You. Help us stay focused on the path to victory. With Your help, we intend to make the most of this cherished second opportunity, to achieve success. We pray this in Your name. Amen."

After a heavy silence, the room exploded into applause. Our muscular enforcer was now enforcing, proclaiming God's word?

The kids stood. As a surprise, they had composed a poem for the occasion. They huddled around eight-year old Abbey, the designated speaker. She said:

"'Our families have gathered in Florida from afar.

It took this special trip to learn who we are.

Disney World and the beach provided a lot of fun.

We all got sunburn, but still enjoyed the sun.

There's just one more story that needs to be told;

The story of our Dads, who will bring home the gold.'"

To fervent applause, Abbey and the others nodded and grinned. It took a lot of courage for her to speak. After hearing her words, I felt nothing would stop us from our quest.

The dinner and festivities took several hours. Everyone had a wonderful time, with uninterrupted buzz and chatter. For dessert, the waitress brought in a cake boasting our school colors and offering the words, "OUR TEAM–OUR WAY."

Finally, as we were about to leave, a head poked in.

"Gentlemen—see all of you tomorrow. Hey, I can hardly *wait*!"

It was the heckler, the Don Rickles look-alike. We all burst into laughter.

Truly a night to remember! On the way out, Mike stopped by the bar. Unfinished business, he said. We reminded him of game time and wished him luck on his interview. We all caravanned back to our motel and retired early.

We had thought about tomorrow for a long, long time. Within hours it would be upon us.

SEVENTEEN

A WINNER NEVER QUITS
AND
A QUITTER NEVER WINS

T he phone rang, loudly; our 8 a.m. wake-up call. No matter what this last day in Orlando would bring, the memories were destined to live forever. I wondered how Mike was doing; his interview had just started.

"Knowing Mike, I'm sure he's charming the station," said Terry.

I was to meet the guys at 10:45 a.m., so I took Adam for a walk to the children's play area while Terry and Kim got ready. Adam insisted on bringing his rubber foot-long alligator to scare people. It was a beautiful day, with a slight breeze. Predictions were that the noon temperature would reach nearly 90°.

After breakfast, we lounged around until it was time to meet. We assembled in Jim's room. Mike hadn't yet returned. We talked about our poor execution, our inability to stop their man-to-man offense—the 1-4 they had used against us in game one. And their big man, Evans, was a force inside. Again we considered "Chameleon." Playing from behind against this team would be extremely tough, so we would have to focus and stay close. Their ball-handling skills might negate our press. Yet, we were very positive. We had a great chance. If we could just maintain our A game … for the entire contest.

At 11:25 a.m. we headed to the court, and spied Mike running towards us and slipping into his jersey at the same time. We told him to slow down. He had plenty of time. The interview went well; he would know by next week. He had changed in the van on I-4 on the way back from Orlando.

Arriving at the courts, we were swept away by the air of excitement. Music played. A party atmosphere prevailed. The main desk stood by the entrance. Bleachers surrounded Court Four. Playing on Court Four—my favorite number—was a fine omen.

The stands were starting to fill. The Las Vegas fans were decked out in High Flyer shirts. A large banner read "THREE CHAMPIONSHIPS IN A ROW—WAY TO GO!" In the corner sat a live truck from Channel 9 Orlando, accompanied by a male photographer and female reporter.

Mike grinned. "I pitched the story just this morning. They went with it?!" He waved. "Hi, Nicole!" he called to the reporter.

A moment later we ran into Julie, the bartender from Ryan's. She smiled at Mike, gave him a kiss. "Good luck, boys," she said.

"Geez, you know *everybody*!!" said Joe.

We acknowledged our fans beside our bench, each of their matching yellow shirts reading "CHEESE SECTION." The Bunny appeared, in a shirt announcing her as "THE KING'S QUEEN."

As we approached the desk, the heckler stepped up, another gentleman in tow.

"Morning, fellas. Want you to meet my friend Roger—Rodney Dangerfield. Really! Uh, Roger—wanna do your thing?"

Roger viewed our Jerseys, shook his head, put a hand up to his neck as if clutching a tie. "I tell ya! Uniforms like *that, you'll* get no respect either!'"

Everyone laughed. The heckler turned.

"Roger, this is Barb—also known as the Bunny."

Barb stepped close. Roger viewed her shirt—THE KING'S QUEEN. Eyes bulging, he pronounced— "Wow, I'll take one of those. Deliver it to *my* palace—personally!"

Everyone cracked up.

Rex came over. Roger took in his size. "Hey, you must be the *King*! King, I'm just a humble servant—rooting for your team. Wanna make the boys root harder? Have *her* cheerlead."

More laughter.

"Time to take our seats. Come on, Roger."

The two walked off. "Roger, over, and *out*," the other quipped.

At the desk the tournament director assigned us to the east end to warm up. He wished us luck. Approaching our bench, we heard an eruption of cheers from our fans. Several players from the tournament yelled good luck. The two injured Slammers sat together with bandaged foreheads. They nodded, and waved. Behind the bench the kids had constructed a sign—THE SOUTH 20.

We took the floor and had a great warm-up. Everyone seemed to be shooting with confidence. At the other end, the High Flyers, in full force, were preparing briskly. Some fifteen minutes later the horn sounded. This being the championshipgame, protocol called for team introductions and a playing of the National Anthem. As we huddled together one last time, I couldn't help but notice the intense looks marking all our other player's faces. As the last note faded, Craig said, "Guys, we *belong* here. We have a strong, wonderful, talented team—*believe* in each other."

We joined our hands, shouted "1-2-3 *TEAM*!"

The crowd grew frenzied as the teams readied for the center jump. As the refs checked everyone's position, the words sounded:

"Flyers—better be flying *high*. Cuz these guys aren't going to roll over and *die*!!"

Everyone smirked, including both refs.

Dave pointed to Rex. "*His* dad," he announced.

Rex could only shake his head.

The ref readied himself, tossed the ball. It was now time—time to take what was ours and regain our pride.

Their 6'9" center Evans got the tip. Quickly the Flyers set their offense against our man-to-man, running a four-man motion with Evans, a real load inside, moving block to block. They were signaling; look to pound the ball inside. It took four passes to get him the ball on the right block. He faked to the middle, then came back with a sweet jump hook that kissed off the glass: 2-0.

"Way to gooooo, Flyers!" someone yelled.

Craig inbounded the ball quickly to Dave, while the three of us ran our lanes. We rushed the ball up court. But their transition defense was sound, and we moved to our secondary break. This they foiled as well, and we had to pull the ball back out and reset. I remembered. We had been able to score only twice on fast breaks in our game against them.

Like us, the Flyers came out in a man-to-man defense. Seeing how tightly my man was playing me, Dave tapped his head as a cue for me to go backdoor. Rex rushed to the high post, I to the wing. Dave faked the ball to me perfectly. I immediately changed direction sharply into a backdoor cut. Dave squared up, threw the lead pass perfectly. I laid it: 2-2.

Our fans erupted, but a moment later the Flyers answered with a long corner three. We brought the ball down, ran motion. It took us seven passes before Craig made his move toward the hole, bringing help from Mike's man and kicking it back out to Mike at the top of the key. The net barely moved as he knocked down the shot.

For the next several minutes each team mirrored the other. On our next two possessions Rex faced up on the block, hit a short jumper, then attacked the rim with a reverse flush. This he did at the expense of Evans, who incurred his first foul. When the Flyers started to double- team Rex, we attacked the other side, running a pick-and roll with Mike and Craig. Craig set a ball screen, quickly slipped to the hole, received Mike's great pass, and responded with a thunderous dunk.

Thirteen minutes in the half and the Flyers led, 16-15. Since his initial goal, Evans had not gotten another opportunity. Rex was fighting him tooth and nail for lane position. On one occasion, Evans leaned against Rex in the post, preparing his move. Rex simply moved back, separating himself, and Evans fell to the floor, off-balance—a traveling violation. It looked as if someone had pulled a chair out from under him.

However, his teammates picked up the slack, countering with some spectacular moves and sticking their jump shots. With the game so close, we wondered who would be first to give in and try something different?

We were up 21-19 when the Flyers shifted into a zone defense. They went to what seemed to be a 1-3-1 but after the first pass changed into a 2-1-2. They were disguising the defense. Luby had taught us to watch the first pass as the key.

Quickly we changed from our box set to our two-guard (gap-hold) alignment, and hit pay dirt. Using Craig in the short corner, we broke the game open. In the next four possessions, we hit a short jumper and two threes. The Flyers countered only once, with a fast-break lay-up off a long rebound. With us in front, 29-21, the Flyers called a time-out.

Our crowd cheered and whistled loudly as we approached the bench. "Stay with it, guys!" yelled the Bunny. At once all our families rose, into a standing ovation.

We knew we should look for a change when we came out. But we decided to stay in our help man-to-man defense. Wasn't the old adage, "If it ain't broke, don't fix it"? We took the floor to find the Flyers in a full court 1-2-1-1 zone press. We in-bounded, smartly got the ball to the middle with the second or third pass, and flawlessly moved into the forecourt. When Craig completed the possession with a thunderous dunk, the crowd erupted. Their press hadn't fazed us. In fact, we loved it.

After four attempts, they abandoned the press. It seemed we had answered the call and they were on their heels, in need of an answer. They took a timeout to seek a solution. They certainly found one. They went back to a man-to-man and increased their aggressiveness big time. On offense, they dropped their four-man motion and went to their 1-4 set-up, with four people on the baseline and their talented point guard at the top of the key. As in game one, their exceptionally quick guard would start each possession by breaking Dave down on the dribble. This they should have realized earlier—it was the set-up that had taken such a toll on us in the first game. Luckily, they had not. But with five minutes to go in the half, we were up 33- 29.

The momentum had turned. Their quickness was breaking us down. Their offensive scheme was hampering our ability to help one another. Additionally, on offense we were getting poor shots. At one point, Dave had been obliged to launch a long air ball in an effort to beat the shot clock—which gave them the ball out of bounds. "Air ball! Air ball!" the Flyer fans had chanted as we had retreated on defense.

We wanted to make it to intermission with our man-to-man, so as not to show our hand and give them time to discuss a change. We slowed our offense, made at least seven passes to make them work on defense. This tactic took us out of our natural rhythm, and we missed our next four shots without grabbing an offensive rebound. We were close to panicking. Each one-and-done possession was giving them more confidence.

As the half drew to a close, the Flyers brought the ball down, leading 36-33. At seven seconds, they penetrated from the top and kicked the ball out to a wing. Joe did a super job contesting, and the three-point attempt bounced high to the side. Dave jumped, grabbed the ball, and took off down the court, three seconds remaining. The Flyers' point guard ran with him neck and neck. As they sped across half court, Dave took a final dribble to the right and, with an Allen Iverson move, crossed the ball over to his left hand, leaving the opponent to run right past him. He gathered himself and rose for the jumper from what appeared to be about thirty-eight feet. The ball arched high—and swished through the basket as the horn sounded. Dave had put a dagger right in their hearts.

Cheers erupted, persisted. In our bid for the national championship we were once again tied with the Flyers, with fifteen minutes to go. As we reached the bench, our fans were still cheering.

As the noise ebbed, we heard it, "Way to go, runt! Who's *your* daddy…. the King?"

We turned, peeked back. Now Roger, too, had edged in, eyes bulging, fingers tugging his collar—

"Hey come on! *That* puts the R in *REEE*-spect!"

The crowd gave them a hand. The two elevated their

arms as if to quiet the crowd, and sat back down. It was truly a circus atmosphere.

The first half had been clean. Only Rex and Mike had two fouls. The Flyers were in equal shape foul-wise. We agreed. The best thing that had happened was their going into a zone in both full- and half-court. That decision—and our ability to react to it with confidence—had allowed us to keep the game close, especially against this more athletic group. We would not be seeing any of that any time soon—this we knew. What concerned us the most was their 1-4 offense. In an effort to counter, we would play some alternating zones. We finished our water and heard the loudspeaker: "Two minutes."

When we stood up we were astonished to find a familiar figure—yes, Shirley, Coach's wife—waving to us. "Hi, boys. Made it."

"Coach, too?" said Mike.

She pointed. "There—"

We peered over, and stared. At the end of the bench was Luby, seated in a wheelchair. His figure was motionless, but the crooked smile was unmistakable.

We hurried over, greeted him. It had been … twelve years? He was now … seventy-six!

We mumbled hellos, grabbed his hand, hugged him. He didn't say much, but he smiled and nodded his approval.

The horn sounded, summoning us onto the court. "Sit tight," we said. "We'll see you right after the game."

We stalked out. I glanced back. The smile remained.

Joe and Mike hugged Shirley, and took their spots back on the bench.

"I noticed you're playing on Court *Four*!!" Shirley called to me with a smile.

EIGHTEEN

HAVE CONFIDENCE IN YOUR ABILITY AND RESPECT FOR YOUR OPPONENTS

I can only guess how the other guys felt, but I recall having more than just a few butterflies as the second half began. As the ref made his way out onto the court, I spied Terry and Barb hugging Shirley and then Coach. The ref gave the ball to the Flyers to inbound. "Good luck, men," he announced.

Evans easily got the ball to their point guard, but Jim stepped in, tipped it away, and ran the ball down. Dave came and took it from his hands. They were still in man-to man, as we had anticipated. Dave called "In," and Jim and I exited to opposite wings crossing on the baseline, letting me receive the pass from Dave on the left wing with my man several feet away. As my defender ran at me, I pump faked, he bit, and I passed him on the dribble, towards the elbow. When Craig's man rushed up from the low post to help, I bounce-passed it to Craig at the block, who turned and made a short jump hook. We were up, 38-36.

We sprinted back and set up a 1-3-1 zone, with Dave at the top and Jim running the baseline. They set up just as we would, in a box set. Dave worked the "kitchen" area to keep the ball from moving easily from side to side on top. As the ball reached the corners, Mike, responsible for the baseline, sprinted out to cover. While a fine passing team, the Flyers lacked patience against a zone, and were content to take the first good shot. Unfortunately, their attempts were right on—they hit two three-pointers.

Meanwhile, their defense was suffocating. When they overplayed our cuts, we ran counters. Even though they initially overcompensated, their defensive quickness gave them the ability to reestablish their positions and stay with us. Soon we were beginning to exhaust our special plays. After made baskets, the Flyers used a full court man-to-man to create an up-tempo game. As we got the ball inbounds to Dave, he responded like a machine, bringing the ball up the court flawlessly, keeping his body between his defender and the ball.

Against our 1-3-1 the Flyers set a two-guard front, with Evans moving from block to high post to block. They would penetrate the natural gaps and kick the ball to a teammate. They always looked for Evans. The last time they found him on the dotted line, and he responded with a Kareem-style hook that barely rippled the net. To crimp Jim's ability to make his way across the baseline and cover the corners, they set screens on the baseline. It worked, and the corner shot became available for them.

We switched to a 2-1-2 zone to give them another look. They shifted to a one-guard front and utilized a short corner very well. With their tough man-to-man defense and our altering defenses, the score remained low. It took several passes to find a shot opportunity for both teams. This was a plus for us. If the score stayed low, we had a much better chance of success. Also, the zone defenses were giving us fine rebounding positions and mostly limiting them to one shot.

It was becoming a dogfight, with offensive patience a critical factor for both teams. They were adjusting to our shifting defensive schemes and were starting to have more success. With eight minutes left to go they made a 15-foot bank shot, which gave them a 7-point lead. We called a timeout. I suggested a change. We couldn't allow any wider difference in the score. "Guys, trust me," I said. "We need to run Chameleon, give them another look they haven't seen. We have eight minutes—maybe ten to fifteen defensive battles— left." Joe agreed. "He didn't get his nickname 'Coach' for nothing. Let's go with Rick's instincts. Let's *do* it."

We agreed to go with "Chameleon." At this point I could not help but again note the similarities between the Flyers and Central Wisconsin of eighteen years before. We mirrored each other in size, were having difficulty executing offense, and were giving them control at the right time—all in the most important game of the year. Maybe because the last two teams we had ever lost to were Central and the Flyers? The Flyers were becoming our new Central, it seemed. Had they seen us once too often and figured us out? We had talked of defensive responsibilities in "Chameleon," but never tested them in a game. We *could* make the transition, I believed. I had found the play at a coaching clinic in Seattle a year before. A Coach Veltri had touted its merits. We were about to test his theory. With eight minutes to go we were taking a chance, a *big* chance.

We stepped out onto the floor determined to make it work, lining up in a 1-2-2 defensive set with Craig at the point. To counter, the Flyers went to a two-guard box set. When they did, Craig retreated to the lane area to give us a

2-1-2 look and put them in an improper set. As they shifted into a one-guard alignment with two wings, a post, and a short corner, Craig sprinted back up to the point to give us the 1-2-2 look again and negate their setup. Our constant change left our defense similar to an accordion, with its flexing movement. The defense had some match-up-zone principals which the guys picked up on quickly and still provided us with fine rebounding positions.

"Chameleon" paid swift dividends. The Flyers turned the ball over on their first possession on a shot-clock violation. With a few seconds on the shot clock but no possible chance, their point guard passed to their three man in the corner. With the clock down to virtually zero, it seemed like he had been handed a grenade with the pin already pulled. On their second possession, they missed a short, contested shot. We were working the new defense as if we had practiced it for years. The guys grew more excited, as their efforts met with success. We were taking a risk, yes, but it was a calculated one.

With six minutes to go, we cut their lead to 52-50. Then their two-guard, Williams, hit a long three with Joe draped all over him. We came right back and ran "X" as our wings exited for the entry pass in a crossing motion, which opened Craig for a short jumper on the baseline.

It was amazing how well we had been running our sets this tournament. Compared to the other teams, we seemed so organized and so attentive to detail. For this we had no one to thank but the man seated at the end of our bench.

As Las Vegas brought the ball down and went into the post, Romeo was able to strip the ball, retrieved it, and get it to the Midget. We brought the ball down, set the offense. "W!" shouted Dave. We would do a weave. We three on the perimeter weaved the ball as Craig and Rex crossed, screened in the lane. This was a play we enjoyed, as we knew they would not switch defensively. Handing the ball off to each other on the dribble legally screened the defender out of the play. The result was an elbow J by Jim.

The Flyers now led, 55-54, with three minutes to go. Both teams took extreme care with their final possessions. Both, however, missed on the next two opportunities, leaving the Flyers up by a single point and bringing the ball down with 1:12 remaining. As their point guard penetrated, Dave caught him on the arm, sending him to the line for the bonus. He made his first shot, but his second bounced off to Dave, who had screened out the free-throw shooter. We were down by two, with 1:05 left. Deciding not to take a timeout and save the two we had, Dave pulled the ball out to organize us, then called "Curl! " I circled right around Rex, received a pass from Dave, and banked a short jumper off the board. The score was now 56-56.

The crowd broke into applause. Everyone was now standing and cheering. The clock showed 43 seconds as the Flyers brought the ball down and set their offense. To avoid a violation, they would have to shoot with 17 seconds left. They got the ball to Evans at the post. He squared up, pounded the ball on the floor, and made a strong move to the right block. Rex stopped his penetration, hugged up to him, and, with arms stretched, traced the ball. The big center could do nothing but fan it off to their shooter, Williams, in the right corner. He got into his shot quickly, as Joe was approaching. The shot bounced off the rim, and Craig secured the rebound. He was immediately hacked by Evans, drawing a whistle. As they were not yet in the penalty, we were awarded the ball out of bounds.

Fourteen seconds left: We took a timeout, and the crowd cheered louder. We would advance the ball to half court as quickly as possible and take our final timeout. This way we would avoid the full-court man-to-man pressure and leave ourselves enough time at the other end. We ran Scatter. I in-bounded the ball with my teammates all lined up at half-court. The ref handed me the ball. I yelled, "Go!" to our players, and they all moved in preconceived direc-tions, a play very difficult to defend. I spied the Undertaker, hook-passed him the ball at about half-court on the right sideline. He leapt, clutched the ball, called for time. Thirteen seconds: Only one second had come off the clock.

Our last timeout; cheers erupted as we came off the court. As we huddled, I peered up. Only a few feet away, Shirley and Coach appeared to be listening and smiling. "Guys, if we run Go-5," I said, "we will walk out of here as champions. We've been saving it. Now is the time."

It was unanimous. We truly had saved it, running it only twice in the tournament, and never against the Flyers. We discussed our roles, which side we would attack. Hopefully, this play would open up their defense just like the Red Sea. We stood, clasped hands. We knew we had to trust one another. "1-2-3… *finish!*" we said.

"Boys—"

We turned. Shirley had edged over to us. "Coach just told me, 'In this particular situation, flip-flop the one and two man.'"

For a moment we stood there, stunned. Just *like* at Lakefield? I told the team; I would come and get the ball. Dave would take my spot on the block, as if the order had come from Coach himself. Indeed, it had, this time through Shirley. Again it was to be the Lavern and Shirley show.

As we lined up, I noticed that Dave's man was at least six inches taller than he was. We inbounded the ball, maneuvered to our spots. I faked inside, ran up to Dave at the top of the key, and he carefully handed me the ball. That put Rex on the right elbow, with Dave on the block below him. On the other side, at the left elbow, was Craig, while Jim stood on the left block behind him. I was holding the ball about three feet above the top of the key. My defensive man was jabbing in and out at me to keep me off balance. Nine seconds on the clock? I squared up. "Go-5!" I yelled. "Go-5!" I foot-faked. My defender retreated a step. I squared back, ripped the ball through, quickly dribbled to the right foul line extended. As I made my way to the wing, Dave spun and set a back-pick on the man defending Craig at the opposite high-post elbow. At that point, my defensive man, sprinting along, caught up to me as I picked up my dribble and squared to the basket. He was all over me, tracing the ball, yelling "Dead, dead, dead!"

When Dave's screen was set, Craig reverse-pivoted and scampered to the low post-position Dave had just vacated. He jump-stopped above the block, hands high, his elbows extended, stance wide, and knees bent—a ready catcher position. I could also see that Rex had joined Dave to set a staggered double screen for Jim near the opposite block. Having already faked his man away, Jim was curling off the set of screens and moving hard to the free-throw area. As the seconds ticked, I could hear the crowd growing louder and louder. I was now getting a fine look at both our options.

It was now that I realized this *was* the same scenario we had faced against Central Wisconsin. That tipped pass had sealed our fate. Dave had been matched against a defender far taller. Now I was assigned the task. If I were to deliver to Craig or Jim, it would be my responsibility to pass the ball to his "sweet spot." It was up to *me* to erase this memory.

I held the ball firmly in two hands, raised it over my head. My opponent raised both hands high to counter. I faked a high pass, and he went up on his toes to defend. I stepped across his body with my left foot and threw a wraparound hook pass to Craig. I threw the ball hard at the floor closer to me than to Craig, and threw it with spin, so that the pass's angle would have it end up waist high in his midsection and allow him to maintain his position. The pass was dead-on. Craig grabbed the ball, secured it firmly, and chinned it. For a second he hesitated, turning his head to survey the defense.

His defender was just arriving as Craig made his move. With a hard dribble he stepped to the middle, keeping his right foot as his pivot foot, and faked a left-handed jump hook. The defender hugged up, hands high, and jumped to block the attempt. Craig gathered the ball with both hands, turned with his left foot across the defender's body, and stepped through. As the defender re-established himself, Craig was at point-blank range to use his right—his strong hand, with the defender on his back. The clock was at 2 seconds. Craig elevated. With his left hand as a shield, he arched the ball high off the glass—right over the other's outstretched hand. I could hear screaming as the ball kissed the glass, caromed off, and dropped right through the basket, scarcely rippling the net.

We had run "Go-5"—brilliantly. As Evans clutched at the ball, the horn sounded. We had earned the victory. National Champs?! All six of my teammates pointed to me in gratitude. Then we ran to Craig to congratulate him on his outstanding move and shot.

Fans mobbed the floor. "Way to go, Craig!," "Great, pass, Rick!," "You guys played great!," and "Champs!" echoed and re-echoed. The Bunny jumped up and down, drawing enough attention on her own. Julie the bartender ran up, planted a big kiss on Mike, and announced—"Drinks are on me!" Already WFTV Channel 9's Nicole and her crew were filming crowd reactions and comments from the players. Terry ran up with a big kiss and hug, as did all the wives, The kids lifted their banner, then flipped it over. "2007 CHAMPS!" it read.

We seven regrouped, as a sign of unity. How fitting that Craig, our captain of faith, had scored the winning basket! We lifted our hands, joined them together. "Thank you, Lord, for this wonderful time," said Craig. "I guess Rest in Peace wasn't such a bad name after all?" said Joe. "Sure glad you made that pass, Rick," Dave threw in. "I certainly wouldn't have if Coach hadn't flip-flopped us," I confided.

Coach and Shirley had wide smiles. Somehow Coach remembered the difficulty Dave had incurred in 1989 and didn't want history to repeat itself. His being here at exactly the right time for us seemed to be destiny, divine timing. He had been here for only a short hour, and once again had influenced our lives.

We congratulated the Flyers on their effort, then made our way to Coach. We told him how much we appreciated his insight, his presence.

As the director announced the trophy presentation, the crowd quieted down. The Flyers drew a protracted round of applause as they received their trophy. Even in defeat they were a class act—Flyers indeed.

When our turn came, we wheeled Coach out to receive our trophy. He accepted it, held it high to the sounds of still more cheers. The Magnificent Seven had its "Shining Moment"—at last.

A pair of voices broke out. "Okay, ya hockey puck! Let's crown the King and kiss the Queen!" said one. "Last time I was this excited, my fourth wife-to-be cancelled the wedding!" called the other. "No respect, I tell ya!"

The crowd broke into hysterics, and began to clap in rhythm. The two men took long, deep bows, and retired.

We took the trophy. There, before all, we presented it officially to Coach. "Eighteen seasons late, Coach, but this—is for you," announced Dave. "Just, um, sorry it *took* so long?!"

We all yelled, clapped heartily. With a visible tear in his eye, Coach looked up and gave us a wink.

At Rex's suggestion, we resolved how the $10,000 check would be spent. Unanimously we decided to use it for the Jim Freemont Scholarship Fund. He *would* finish his degree. The Magnificent Seven would all be college grads.

Once more we convened around Coach, and knelt. As he held up the trophy for a final time, we posed. The Bunny screamed "Cheese!"—and snapped the photo.

Epilogue

Most go their own way after their college days are complete, even when the proximity between friends is minimal. Into their lives come new challenges, desires, changes. Our group, too, had followed this well-trodden path—for some eighteen years. Then, out of who-knows-where, some force had awakened in us to convince us to reassemble. Why? To attend to unfinished business? The common denominator was our experience as team members at Lakefield College. Coach Lubinski had been the catalyst. He had originally brought us there and had been a mentor influencing us far, far beyond the game of basketball. That we seven have met with success, each in his own way, traces back to the life skills taught us by Coach. His faith, his genuineness, and his love of the entire human family—these together were his m.o. Basketball and math were his vocation. He used the principles of each to develop life-long skills for his athletes. These seeds of growth not only blossomed but spread into a kindred spirit in all of those he touched. Someone once asked the great sculptor Michelangelo how he created a piece of art. He replied that the sculpture already existed within the marble. His job, as he saw it, was to rid the excess marble that surrounded this wonderful creation. Coach had the same philosophy. He worked each day to shape us and lead us to realize our potentials.

I consider myself fortunate to have been guided by Lavern Lubinski. It is the duty of each coach or supervisor to guide those on the team or organization to success and to help each grow as an individual. I guess we could say—Luby just kicked this up a notch!

If you want to build a program—be it basketball or business—consider the Lubinski Method. It starts with faith and hard work. It is nurtured by ethics. It oozes integrity.

We Magnificent Seven followed this path and have come to love this path. Our journey continues ...

A TESTAMENT
OF TIME

Composing this novel was an exciting and emotional time for me. I could hardly wait to mail a copy to Coach Luebstorf. Although this book is primarily a work of fiction, the character of Coach Lubinski is based on the life and values of Lavern Luebstorf, a legendary Wisconsin coach, and is truly the motivation behind this story. Two months elapsed before I received a response. The following is an excerpt from his reply:

Dear Rick,

First of all, I am utterly disgusted with myself for taking so long to acknowledge your unbelievable gift to me. If truth be told, I was actually rather afraid to write. I didn't know what to say that could come close to the emotional pull that your book had on me. I literally broke down even before I began reading. How can I ever begin to repay you for all the kind things you said about me? All I can humbly say is 'Thank You' from the bottom of my heart. I read Go-5 from start to finish the first time through. I couldn't turn the pages fast enough. It seemed like I knew everyone. The characters were very real, distinct in their own ways, each having an attraction that made me want to know them better. I couldn't believe that the book would end when you suffered your first defeat. It had to go on—and it did! And I was there for the thrilling ride all the way to the championship. It showed me that if a person dreams and, for whatever reason that dream doesn't come true, don't stop dreaming—start a new dream. More than once, I had to set the book aside, but only for a few moments to pause, reflect, wipe away a misty tear or two, before rushing on. I wanted to rush to the ending, but I wanted to linger and enjoy the special moments along the way. After I finished, I had a good long talk with myself. I have been so richly blessed in having known so many young people, as they progressed through life. And, of course, all my co-coaches who never received the acclaim that they should have received and richly deserved. Basketball has always been and always will be a rich component in my life.

Next, I decided to re-read Go-5, but this time I forced myself not to hurry and to reflect and to identify. I only allowed myself one chapter a day, but I made each chapter last for hours. The fine line between truth and fiction went back and forth. I was engrossed in the pursuit. Even though I knew how the book was going to end, it made no difference to my enjoyment. It was a thrill going along on the ride, meeting old friends along the way and renewing recent acquaintances. Rick, it was so beautiful. I was re-born, practicing once again as a young boy, imaging last-second winning heroics, goose pimples, and a time of peaceful harmony. And now, as I am an older person, still the ball only bounces up......

During the course of the golf season I get to play with perhaps a dozen or so of my former players at different sites in the state. I really look forward to these occasions, not because of golf but because I can marvel at how they have matured into great citizens. And the amazing thing is that even though some have entered their 50s, they are still boys with dreams of playing basketball again. Rick, I don't think they will ever give up that lingering feeling of the soft touch that flows through your fingertips on that pure shot that brings you nothing but net....

A few basketball seasons ago, at one of the school games, I was honored. There were players from every team I had ever coached. It was a moving and humbling experience. I got to renew old times with them at a reception afterwards. Many of them that you co-coached asked me about you and told me *how much you added to their game. I told them that basketball will forever be part of your life, that even though you have moved miles away memories do not have a time or distance barrier.*

Rick, you have contributed so much to so many in your life. Loving father, loving husband, wonderful friend, peerless coach. Thank you for being part of my life. Thank you for the totally undeserving dedication. Perhaps, some day once again, we shall be able to get together once more to relive and re-love those golden moments.

Go-5,

Lavern Luebstorf

Lavern's response overwhelmed me. Coach always had a unique way of using "special or hidden messages or meanings" woven into a lesson. Again he delivered another knockout punch, as only he could do. His letter demonstrated his selfless service, compassion, and dedication to, most importantly, the growth of his former student-athletes.

Yes, we dream of the game with the pure love of a young child. But if, for whatever reason, our dreams don't come true, we must never give up—we must start a new dream. Still the ball only bounces up....

BASKETBALL INDEX

General Tips

•Mastery of skills through the use of fundamentals invites physical achievements; victory is visualized and the power to relax comes naturally.

•Possession of the ball is a fundamental of the game itself. You can't score without it; the other team can't score if you have it. Get the ball, keep it, pass it, possess it.

•A teammate may be faster than you; he may be a better shot or a more clever passer; he may be a better defensive player; and he may be taller and heavier—but he should not be superior in team spirit, fight, determination, ambition, and character.

•A well-conditioned team is necessary to any degree of efficiency.

•There are no short-cuts to being a well-conditioned team.

•Good training is the observance of everything and anything that makes for good physical and mental condition.

•Eating habits must be good. Don't eat sweets. Don't substitute them for wholesome foods. Eat a good breakfast.

•Sleep is the master builder of our bodies.

•Observance of training rules come from within a player; it cannot be forced.

•Personality and character develop through sacrifice, hard work, and observances of training rules.

•Basketball surpasses all college games in terms of teamwork. In basketball, every player should receive the ball continually during an offensive movement in the scoring zone.

•Passing is basketball's most important fundamental.

•Basketball requires speedy footwork, leg spring (hops), timing, and endurance—so work to develop these traits.

•Handling the ball is the key to a high–class basketball team.

•A team is in no grave danger if it possesses and knows what to do with the ball.

•Knowing when not to shoot is just as important as knowing when to shoot.

•The game of basketball is not only a privilege but a responsibility.

•Many, many millions attend basketball games each year.

•Plays are important, but players who have not mastered the fundamentals will never be able to execute plays.

•An athlete confident in his ability to execute fundamentals will show poise on the floor.

•"Basketball is an easy game to play, but difficult to master."— Dr. Naismith

•Like any other science, to know basketball well one must have a thorough knowledge of its principles. Sweeping generalities will not do. Vague instruction will prove fatal.

•Defense: Footwork and condition are to the defense what passing and shooting are to the offense.

•Passing: No player should be on the team who cannot pass.

•Morale, poise, and the will to succeed mark a winning combination.

•A basketball player should have the following qualities:

speed, skill, game knowledge, conditioning, and courage.

•Be mentally alert and aggressive on defense.

•A job poorly done stands as a witness against the man who does it.

•Determination to outplay your opponent, to shut him out, to get the rebounds, to be a great ball-hawk, to do more than your part towards a good team defense brings out the best in a player.

•Determination, fight, and mental and physical aggressiveness are necessary to a solid defense.

•A team's defense can only be as strong as its weakest individual.

•Overconfidence robs a player of mental and physical aggressiveness.

•A player is of little value to a team if his man scores as many points as he does.

•Basketball still has two departments—offense and defense.

•Win honestly and with modesty. Lose courageously and without whimpering.

•Never be satisfied with your present development.

•Superior ability gained through long periods of training far outdoes mediocre preparation.

•A coach has done well when he has built character as well as a team.

•To succeed, a team must have a spirit of cooperation, a give-and-take attitude, a respect for each other's ability, and a feeling of friendliness and helpfulness between players and the coach.

•A half-hearted effort never wins a place on a squad.

•A good athlete should be determined to do better and thereby become more proficient.

•There's a lot of space in the world for a winner, but a "Standing Room Only" sign is always up for the loser.

•A desire to play as a team, to submerge the self for the benefit of the group, to attain perfection, to put their powers to the utmost, and to win will turn a mediocre team into a team of poise, judgment, and determination.

•Anger is a decided enemy of true basketball. Where there is more anger there is less relaxation and concentration. Anger prevents the clear-mindedness needed for reflective and reflexive actions in game conditions.

•A player's experience allows that it is necessary to adjust to a variety of playing conditions.

•Great competitors do not permit little things to affect their performances.

•Good conditioning means greater efficiency, accuracy, and endurance.

•Great physical conditioning and no competitive fiber would be as bad as poor conditioning and a great, competitive heart.

•Lack of sleep means less muscular relaxation, drains the body of its power to make needed repairs.

•Solid free-throw shooting is a great stabilizing influence. The ability to convert a high percentage of free throws will keep a team in the game when its shooting from the floor is lackluster.

•It is a greater compliment to have it said about you "He is hard to guard" than "He is a great shot."

•A temperature of about 60° is best for play.

•Confidence and practice is half the battle in free-throw shooting. Practice will improve free-throw accuracy and thus breed confidence.

•A strong defense is a stabilizing factor. It enables you to stay within reach of your opponent and prevent your own disorganization.

•Officiating varies greatly. Accept calls without criticism. Adjust to the officiating.

•Most close games are lost by mistakes of the head more than mistakes of the hands or feet. Everything hinges on the little things.

•It is my very pleasant duty to help place my players in good jobs upon their graduation. My duty does not end after that first job. Contact with the former players should always be close, and I stand ready and eager to help my former players advance in their chosen professions.

•The more that players understand the objectives of the game, the more valuable they are to the team.

•Fundamental drills should be a segregated part of practice. Use this time to develop footwork, hand-eye coordination, timing, and confidence.

•A player's greatest team value may very well be his rebounding—go get that ball!

•Knowledge of the game makes for confidence.

•Players should be not only conformers but transformers.

•An athletic team on a trip represents the school. Faculty, students, and alumni want the school represented in a way that brings credit. This is the responsibility of a coach and players.

•Keep tall players on the floor on out-of-bounds plays.

•The free-throw shooter is responsible for the defensive positions of his team during the free throw.

•The champion's psychological profile includes ambition, psychological endurance, competitiveness, coachability, organization skills, team orientation, aggression, hidden reserves, character, ability to perform under pressure, leadership, courage, a take-charge attitude, intelligence, hard work, poise, and physical toughness.

•Any time you can fake your opponent out of position and go by, do so.

•If stalling and you receive a pass, look behind you.

•Follow-through applies to both passing and shooting.

•Dominate your opponent.

•Be determined to outplay and outscore your opponent.

•You will make mistakes; make every effort not to repeat them.

•Basketball teams are made during the off-season.

•To avoid being a poor loser—WIN!

•Have confidence in your ability and respect for your opponents.

•Do your best to make yourself and every other member of your squad the best possible players.

•If you are a substitute, try to be the best possible substitute.

•Study the game. Learn all there is to know about it. Knowledge is power!

•Qualities of a good team include mastery of such fundamentals as fakes, reverses, change of pace, shooting, guarding on defense, reserve strength, mental poise, courage, team spirit, and faith.

•Constant practice and training produces skill, which may offset mere physical ability.

•Keep the ball moving.

•Don't force your passes.

•Don't pass in front of your opponent's basket.

•Don't start every move by dribbling the ball.

•Drive as much as possible.

•Practice every fundamental at game speed.

•Keep your head up.

•Always be ready to pass and cut.

•Always be ready to shoot.

•No system is good enough to offset poor training habits, poor conditioning, or sharpness.

•Attitude and mistakes will defense your team more than will any opponent.

•The player possessing the ball becomes the offensive captain. He starts the rhythm of the offense.

•Offensively and defensively, act with a purpose.

•If an individual has a fine attitude, it is much easier to draw from that desire, dedication, responsibility, and dependability. He will more easily become a competitor.

•Offensively: Keep constant pressure on the defense after a rebound, interception, basket, or turnover.

•The best time to score on an opponent is in transition, as they change from offense to defense.

•Defensively: Pressure the offense until they cannot establish their game. Individually, keep your man from establishing his rhythm, forcing him out of the things he does best. Have pride in your defensive progress.

•If you think on a basketball floor, it is too late. You must learn to react.

•Don't be too anxious to defend your actions. You must be able to laugh at your own mistakes.

•Always look for positive things about your team and your teammates. Let the coach judge your team's abilities.

•Start practice with enthusiasm. End practice with a desire to practice longer.

•Regardless of the time or the situation, always utilize fast-break possibilities.

•Learn to accept the bitter with the sweet. If criticized, consider the source. Don't let criticism hinder your progress or enhance the tremendous benefits athletics offer.

•Remember: The proper training habits of a fine athlete are habits to establish for life.

•Being able to put the ball in the basket may camouflage your team's deficiencies.

•Don't play too fast.

•Recognize change.

•Meet challenges.

•Be confident in yourself, your teammates, your coaches.

•Recognize "the particular situation."

•Leave the game on the floor.

•Breaking a full-court press does not always require a fast break.

•Be strong with the basketball.

Offensive Tips

•Attempt to hurry the ball into the quarter-court on every possession.

•Normally, look to get the ball inside first, to create a sag situation for the defense. Then attack from the perimeter when it opens up and the shot presents itself.

•Generally speaking, eight baskets per half from a set offense should be enough to win a game. Other points will result from transition, second-chance points, and free throws. Execution is the key.

•Your position will be designated by a number in offensive attacks. Know the responsibility of each number. They are largely interchangeable and designed with simplicity in mind.

•Dribble only for the following reasons: to advance the ball up the floor, to improve or create a passing angle, to drive, to score, to relieve pressure, to penetrate a gap, to gather balance or rhythm, to avoid a travel violation.

•Upon receiving the ball, assume a triple-threat position with an inside pivot foot and face the basket.

•When posting up your man on defense, be able to dropstep, jump-hook towards middle, step through, face up, or stab shot. Be open-minded.

•Preserve your dribble so that you can use it most effectively.

•If you possess the ball and your teammates are setting an off-the-ball screen, look for two options—the cutter and the screener.

•If you can beat your man, take the ball to the basket.

•Generally speaking, pass up a shot if someone else has a better one.

•The shot fake is one of the best fakes in basketball.

•Set up all your cuts. The ability to move without the ball is fundamental to offensive success.

•When a shot goes up, cover your rebound area. If you lose possession of the ball, immediately think defense.

•When you catch the ball, always be ready to score.

•After looking at your initial scoring options, quickly penetrate zone gaps to create two-on-one situations.

Shooting Tips

•Relax.

•Be deliberate.

•Keep a comfortable body balance.

•Do not take hope shots. Take sensible shots.

•Gauge the distance.

•Shoot for the basket or the backboard when the angle is available.

•Locate the basket, concentrate, and look.

•Watch the ball until it hits or misses.

•Have a reasonable arc on your shot.

•Follow all shots unless instructed otherwise.

•Practice shooting at game speed.

•Practice only the shots that you would take in a game.

•Start practicing shots close in, then gradually move outward.

•Study the backboard (if you play on a wooden backboard, remember that glass is faster than wood!)

•Keep muscularly coordinated.

•Develop a rhythm.

•Be unselfish. There is enough glory in victory for everyone.

•Square your shoulders to the basket.

•Use your fingertips. Don't let the ball touch the palm of your hand.

•Keep your eye on the front edge of the rim and aim just over it.

•Point your elbow directly at the basket.

•Follow through on your shot.

•Practice shots that are percentage shots.

•You should be able to shoot at close range with either hand with equal ability.

•Always keep your body between the defensive man and the ball.

Pivoting Tips

•Timing is essential in pivoting. A player whose teammate is pivoting must create the timing. Don't come too soon; come late and fast.

•Use pivoting to escape someone guarding you, even if you do not have the ball.

•Practice your change of direction pivots.

•As a general rule, pivot to the outside.

•When pivoting, threaten your opponent, then step through, reverse, and pass.

•When faking a pass, do not move your feet. Keep them square to the opponent and pivot by him.

•Keep low on all pivots. Be ready to drive in any direction after the pivot is made.

•In pivoting, move away from the opponent guarding you when passing to a trailer.

•After you pivot, you may have the ability to run interference. Try to go the same way as the man you have passed. You will then be between the defender and the man whom you have passed to. Also, you may give up the ball to a cutter, pivot, and go in the opposite direction. Doing the latter, you place the defender between yourself and your teammate. If the defender follows the receiver, your teammate may give you a quick return pass.

Defensive Tips

•When your man has the ball, approach him with a boxer or stride stance. If he has the dribble available, close in on him with smaller stutter-shuffle steps. When he moves laterally, slide and square your stance.

•When you are in position on your man and he has not yet dribbled, move in and out at him. Never give him time to plan or rest. Pester him constantly.

•Read your man's eyes, and view his body.

•When your man starts a fake or a dribble, immediately release one-half step, then square up to the ball and slide.

•When your man stops dribbling, immediately smother him and trace the ball.

•Split your man on the strong side.

•When your man passes, immediately release towards the basket and move his cutting path.

•Keep your feet moving. Do not get caught standing still or standing up. Keep alert. Play defense when your man does not have the ball. Do not allow him to receive the ball in an advantageous position.

•After a shot, block your man out, then go after the ball.

•Remember: It is not necessary to touch or block a shot if you constantly pester your opponent.

•Use your feet—not your hands—when you help with team defense.

•Do not reach to either side. Keep your arms close to your sides.

•If you lose your man, go directly to the basket until you

find him, and work your way out toward him.

•See both your man and the ball whenever possible. Point one hand towards your man and the other towards the ball. Keep both in view. If you lose one, lose the ball.

•If you end up on a low post-man, generally side and front him. Do not stand behind him.

•Improve your faking on defense. Remember, the only effective fake is the one that appears real.

•Always pressure the ball.

•When your man does not have the ball, keep him defended, but be more alert to help with team defense.

•Never wait for a man dribbling down the floor rapidly. As he approaches, fake in and out at the ball, then drop off and play tough defense.

•Never relax on defense.

•Make every effort to reduce your fouls without giving up tough, aggressive defense.

•See how fast you can shift from offense to defense.

•Do not leave your feet to block a shot unless the ball is already in the air.

•Force the dribbler away from his strong hand, to a side, or to a congested area.

•Discover the strong and weak points of your man and defend him accordingly.

•Know the system the opponent is running and adjust to it.

•Don't let anyone have an uncontested shot at the basket. Put your hand up on an attempt.

•Generally, do not let an opponent drive the baseline.

•When you feel pride in your defensive accomplishments, you will play better defense.

•Remember that the most effective defense is played before your man gets the ball.

•As a general rule, give your man two-thirds of your attention and the ball one-third.

•Unless you are catching up, never cross your legs. Instead, slide. Don't bob your head.

•Don't charge at an opponent or get your head past your front foot. Keep your body low and advance cautiously. Keep your weight evenly distributed, ready to slide right or left or retreat in either direction.

•After your team has scored and you sprint toward the defensive end, look back over your shoulder.

•Talk on defense. Defense cannot be played without talk. Call out screens and situations as they develop.

•Force your man to commit himself.

•If away from the ball, float. The farther your man is from the ball, the farther you can play away from him.

•Don't come down at the ball on a dribbler or shooter. Come up from underneath.

•Keep opponents from developing an individual or team rhythm.

•Ball-side pressure toughens your team defensively. Help-side defense makes your team succeed.

www.ingramcontent.com/pod-product-compliance
Lightning Source LLC
Chambersburg PA
CBHW060306100426

42742CB00011B/1886